Business Objects

Dashboards

For Beginners

by Paul Bappoo

Paul Bappoo – Business Objects Dashboards for Beginners

A note about the cover images

As well as having a silly obsession with reporting software I am also a fairly keen (amateur) photographer. Having bought myself a "proper grown up" camera I am constantly bothering people and inanimate objects with it. The cover images for this book are no exception. Taken at Terminal 5 of London's Heathrow airport, on one of my many trips through there this year, I decided to take some architectural shots. After about 30 minutes of peering into odd, secluded corners, 3 burly security guards showed up and asked me what I was up to.... they had spotted my suspicious activity on CCTV! I decided to show them what I was taking photos of and about 40 shots into the sequence they either got bored or decided they had better things to be doing and let me get on my way.

About The Author

Email: Paul@Bappoo.com

Web Sites: http://www.BirtReporting.com

http://www.Bappoo.com

 Paul Bappoo has been involved with
Business Intelligence reporting for a
number of years and is the author of
several books and training courses on
the Actuate Business Intelligence and
Reporting Tools (BIRT) product set.
These include the titles: BIRT for
Beginners and BIRT by Example (which are available in paperback
from BIRTReporting.com, Amazon and Barnes and Noble amongst
others) and the BIRT for Maximo Self Study Workbook (which is
available exclusively from
www.birtreporting.com/BIRTTraining.html)
Paul has been an international technical software consultant and
involved with computers for over 30 years. He is a Business
Objects Dashboards Business Intelligence specialist plus regularly

provides services in the field of IBM Tivoli Maximo and Infor SunSystems Reporting and Integration.

Paul runs the BIRT User Group UK and is a member of the BIRT-Exchange Advisory Council.

Companion Web Site

http://www.Bappoo.com

We cover a variety of examples throughout this book, the idea is that you follow the examples and build them yourself. That way you learn the subject matter and internalise it so that it can be readily called upon when you need it in the real world.

However, I know how tricky it can be sometimes to figure something out with a new piece of software, so I have made all the example files, used in the creation of this book, available for free download on my web site.

Feel free to pop along there and register to get access to the downloads, plus get to be one of the first to find out about my latest publications as they are released.

Looking forward to seeing you online.

Contents

A note about the cover images..3

About The Author..4

Companion Web Site.. 6

Foreword... 9

Introduction...11

Install Data Connect 14

Install Business Objects Dashboards.................................... 16

Creating a Web Service.. 17

    Make a connection.. 19

    Create a Query.. 21

    Creating a web service...26

Building a Dashboard... 31

Start a new project.. 32

Overview of design environment... 34

    Menu and Toolbars... 34

Define a Spreadsheet Area.. 42

Connect to the Data Source...43

Adding a Chart.. 48

Filter By Accounting Period.. 55

Adding the Selector..62

Debugging your Dashboard 70

Dynamic Chart Titles.. 78

Spread it around.. 80

Pop Up Drill Downs.. 82

Adding some Style..98

Components... 100

Column Chart Range Finder..100

Tab Control...101

OHLC and Candlestick..102

List Builder...105

Bubble Chart..108

Text Input...111

The Spreadsheet Table..115

The Play Selector...119

Sliders, Dials, Gauges, Line Charts and Alerts......................................123

Understanding the model...126

The Line Chart..129

Sliders...133

Dials...135

Gauges..136

Scorecards...141

Scorecard Alerts...147

Maps...163

Publishing Dashboards...192

Creating a Menu...198

Conclusion..204

BIRT for Maximo 206

BIRT for Beginners...208

BIRT by Example..209

Foreword

I first became interested in Business Intelligence back in 2009, when I attended a Maximo User Group meeting at the IBM Bedfont Lakes facility. Just to put you in the picture, I was working for a software vendor and usually we are not very welcome at user group events because we have a habit of pestering innocent people to buy some software. However, through the good graces of the Maximo User Group organisers I was allowed to attend.

There were a number of exciting software developments that caught my eye at this event, but one of them carried the magic words "Open Source" with it and that was BIRT. Plus it had lots of fancy, Flash based, interactive charts which looked really cool. Well I have spent a lot of time on writing about BIRT and supporting the user community, as well as creating products with it and using it for client implementations. I have always felt that it would be great to look at some alternative software, particularly for the BI Dashboard aspects and when I was given the opportunity to see Business Objects Dashboards, associated with Flynet Data Connect (don't worry I will explain all that stuff later) I thought the combination enabled users to create powerful and graphically rich, interactive dashboards, with great ease.

As usual with any new software product, it takes a bit of effort to get to grips with it and what I specialise in, is learning and understanding a piece of software and then helping others to get up and running with it quickly and easily. Basically, I create the getting started guides that I wish I had when trying to learn a new piece of software.

You should be aware that I have been around in this industry for some time and I see a lot of software. Most of it is absolute rubbish. In the week when I found out about Business Objects Dashboards, I had a detailed look at no less than 3 other products and found them to be compromised and difficult to get to grips with. Dashboards was easy to get results from and being an inherently lazy person, I thought... "That's the one to write about!"

Anyway, I hope this book helps you to be even lazier than me and get up and running and producing impressive results fast. As always I am grateful for any feedback you may have so please feel free to contact me directly on Paul@Bappoo.com

Introduction

Business Objects from SAP has a Business Intelligence module called Xcelsius (well strictly speaking, it is not called Xcelsius any more, we should refer to it as Dashboards). However the reason that it was called Xcelsius, appears to be that it embeds Microsoft Excel as part of the tool that allows you to build dashboards.

So this is the traditional (seems odd talking about the relatively new concept of dashboards as "traditional" but that's the pace of change I guess!) kind of thing you would imagine. A pretty web page, displaying a series of graphs, pie charts and meters, which all jiggle around before settling on their eventual readings which tell you the state of your business at a glance.

What's more, the rather cool looking, Flash based widgets are interactive, so a user can make selections, slide sliders and perform drills with no more than a flick of the wrist and a click of the mouse.

All of this in an easy to use, drag and drop, no developer required paradigm sounds great and mostly the software appears to live up to its claims. There are a few things that I came across when first using the system that are perhaps slightly less than ideal, but there is an active ongoing development process, with an enthusiastic team of developers chipping away at these and sometimes from a not so obvious perspective either.

You see, whilst Dashboards is an SAP product, it cannot natively pull data directly from a database such as SQL or Oracle. It's initial purpose was to create flash objects with built in data. I.e. objects that could be deployed to a web page and then work to interact with each other and the user based on a snapshot of data that was embedded into them at build time. This is where the embedding of Microsoft Excel seems to have come from, because it is that, which allows you to embed data into the Flash objects before they are "compiled" into an swf file for publication.

There is a way to connect these flash object to Crystal Reports server or Business Objects universes and for super large companies, with oodles of technical resource and money to throw at these things, but what we are discussing here is how a small or medium sized business, or indeed a large business that has a desire to save a bit of cash, might wish to use the software.

That was a business opportunity that did not escape the attention of a small but dedicated team of developers, who ran a company called Flynet. They clevery created the Flynet Data Connect software, which allows you and I to easily create a web service (which **can** provide data to Dashboards) in a matter of minutes with the only effort required being the ability to create a SQL statement over the source database. There is even a sql designer of sorts for those of us who prefer not to get our hands dirty with anything that might resemble a programming language.

In this guide, we look at how to install both the Flynet Data Connect software alongside the Dashboards module and then go on to create a dashboard which returns live data from a SQL Server data source. Plus we take a look at the various tools and objects that are available within the software. If you follow this guide from start to finish, within a couple of days you will be proficient at creating great looking dashboards from any major database and you will be obviously deserving of a pay rise!

Install Data Connect

First we are going to install FlyNet Data Connect, start by locating the installation folder and running the DataConnectSetup.exe file.

Next, select Install, this is the large tile in the centre of the dialogue that is displayed.

You will be asked to accept the license agreement, on ticking the check box to indicate that you do, the installation commences.

Next, enter your organization name and licence code.

When the installation is complete, the FlyNet Data Connect Designer launches.

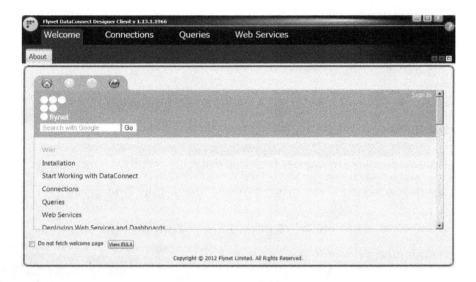

The help pages are displayed and it is worth spending some time reviewing the information available here, there are a number of videos and lots of advice about using the software.

Install Business Objects Dashboards

Next, locate the Dashboard Designer setup program and execute it.

Follow the wizard, accepting the defaults, until you reach the licence screen. Then enter the licence details and continue.

Select the defaults to the end of the wizard and the installation completes.

Creating a Web Service

The first thing you need to do in order to create Dashboards, is set up a web service. The web service comprises two basic parts. Firstly it contains a SQL query which queries the database to return the data you need and secondly it contains the web service side, which is what the Dashboards software will query in order to access the data. The web service is placed into your Microsoft Internet Information Services structure for publication.

Start by launching Data Connect Designer

You will see the welcome screen.

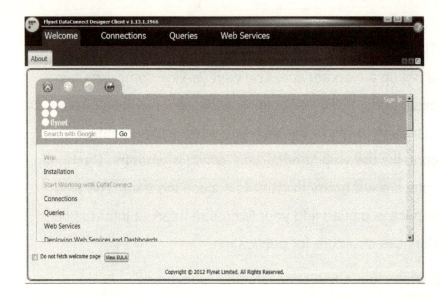

Make a connection

Click on the Connections tab and create a new connection (using the little + sign to the left) with the appropriate connection details.

It is important to use SQL Server authentication, because otherwise the web service will attempt to log on as the APPPOOL account and it is unlikely that this account will have been granted access to your SQL Server.

If you do not wish to use SQL authentication then you either have to give the APPPOOL user access to the database, or turn on 'Impersonation' on the IIS connection. Impersonation impersonates the user of the web service.

To turn on impersonation, you need to click on 'Impersonation' on the IIS connection, and on the web service select 'Windows Authentication'.

If the web service and the database are on different machines, you also need to update Active Directory to allow your machine to 'delegate'.

It is much easier and more reliable to use SQL authentication.

Be sure to test the connection and save the details once you have finished.

Create a Query

The next thing to do is create a SQL query which will return the data you need for the dashboard object that you are about to create. You can create many queries and make them all available as functions of a single web service and basically one connection = one function = one dashboard object (a graph or dial control).

For our example we are going to create a query called SalesByProduct, which will return the value of sales for each product that our company sells. We are reporting against a SunSystems financials database here, but of course you may report against any system of you choice. The basic rule to follow is that your query should not return more than 200 lines of data. Remember, this is dashboard KPI reporting that we are doing here, not long lists of data. So we are aiming to return high level, summarized data.

Whilst there is a query builder within FlyNet Data Connect, I prefer to generate my SQL queries by hand so initially I build them in SQL Enterprise Manager and test that they return the data I am expecting.

Here is my query in detail. You can see that I am returning a summarized value AMOUNT, along with the product code ANAL_T0 and the NAME, which comes from a different table. I am filtering to a specific account code 11000, which in my case is my sales account. I am also checking that the analysis code T0 is not null or blank and then finally I am grouping my result by the product code. Obviously this is a fairly simple piece of SQL code and is an example of the kind of queries that you will need to be writing in order to return high level summarized data.

```
select SUM(AMOUNT) as AMOUNT, ANAL_T0 as ProductCode,
C.NAME

from PK1_A_SALFLDG L

left outer join PK1_ANL_CODE C on L.ANAL_T0 = C.ANL_CODE

where L.ACCNT_CODE = '11000'

and L.ANAL_T0 is not null

and L.ANAL_T0 <> ''

group by L.ANAL_T0, C.NAME
```

In order to create the query in Data Connect, click on the Queries tab and then on the + sign to the left, then enter the details as shown. Select the Connection that you created earlier and then save the query details.

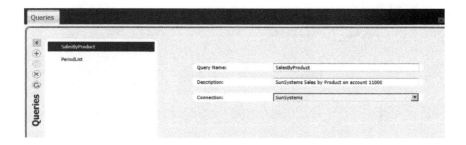

This has defined our query, we now need to fill in the details to make it do something. Click on the D button on the left, to get to the query designer screen.

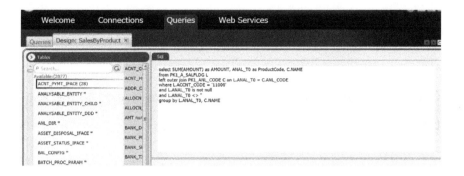

Initially the screen opens with the assumption that you will be using the query builder to create the query in an assisted manner. Since we already have our query, we can simply click the Manual Mode button to access the direct SQL editor.

Now you just need to paste in your code and hit the preview button to see if it works.

Once you are able to successfully test your query, save it and close the Design tab.

Creating a web service

Click on the Web Services tab and click the + sign to the left, then complete the screen as shown.

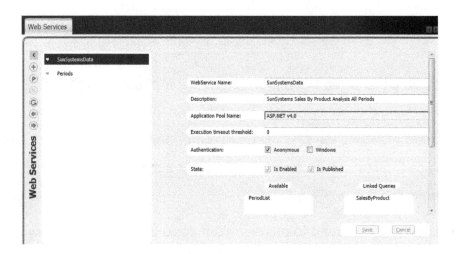

You will notice that the query you created in the previous step is shown in the Available list. Click and drag it to the Linked Queries list, this associates the query to the web service, then click save.

Next we need to publish our web service to the web server. This is achieved by clicking the P button on the left. The published web service screen is displayed and from here we can perform several functions:

- Unpublish the web service

- Update the web service (if we were to make changes to the query for example)

- Disable it for temporary suspension

- View the WSDL

- Test the web service

If you press the test button, you will see a list of all the queries contained in the web service (initially only one) and you can click on the operation to see if it returns data.

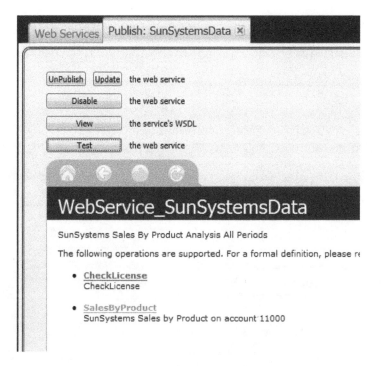

Once you have clicked it, select the Invoke function and you should see a response similar to the following, containing data from the database.

Building a Dashboard

Launch Business Objects Dashboards

Business Objects Dashboards embeds an instance of Excel. Sometimes there can be an error accessing the Excel components. If this happens then close dashboards, close any open Excel sessions and check that there are no Excel processes running in the Task Manager. On re-opening Dashboards the problem should be resolved.

Start a new project

Dashboards initially opens to the start screen.

Click New Blank Model to start a new project and you will
see the design environment screen.

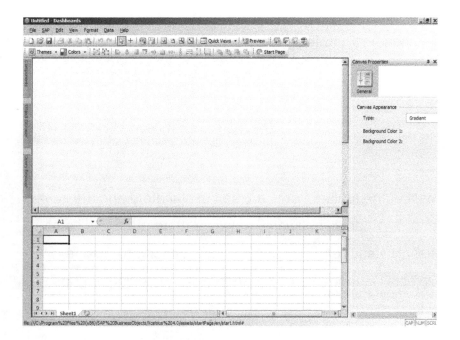

Overview of design environment

Menu and Toolbars

The heading and toolbars

Most of the toolbar items are self explanatory and the same as any Windows software. However there are a few items that are used regularly and are fairly specific to Business Objects Dashboards and therefore worth getting to grips with.

Import Spreadsheet allows you to import an Excel
spreadsheet, which may contain a lot of useful data that can
be used either as the data source for your dashboard or
purely to provide data during the design process. It can be
very useful to have some data on your spreadsheet during
the design so that you can see interactively how your
dashboard is taking shape.

Manage Connections is where you will be spending a lot of
your time when connecting up to external data sources and
mapping those data sources to the spreadsheet, for both
getting data from the spreadsheet as parameters to feed into
your queries and for placing data that comes as the result of
running queries.

Canvas Size Tools allow you to modify the size of the dashboard canvas, either by nudging it larger or smaller or making it fit the components or the window.

You can also set specific sizes, use template sizes and set a global document font from the menu, select **File / Document Properties** to access this screen.

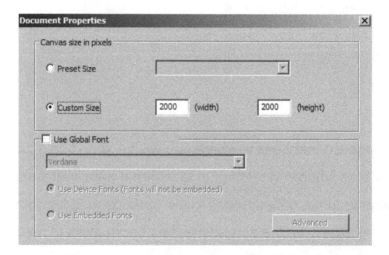

Quick Views allows you to easily switch on and off portions of the main screen. The design area is divided into a number of sections, including a spreadsheet and a design canvass where you lay out the dashboard components. Sometimes you need to focus on just the spreadsheet or just the canvass, so the Quick views allows you to switch between these very quickly.

The preview button will become your good friend, as it is provides instant access to see how your dashboard functions as the end user will see it.

The lower of the two toolbars allows you to group, align and move components under and over each other, along with a button that gets you back to the home screen where you can create new projects.

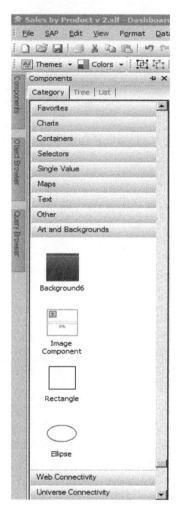

Over on the left hand side are three buttons which will cause a pane to slide out when you hover your mouse over them.

Components are all the objects that you will drag on to your dashboard, such as charts, buttons and backgrounds.

Object Browser lets you see a compact view of all the objects that exist on your dashboard. Clicking an object in the browser selects it on the canvass, this is very useful if you need to, for example, select an object that is underneath other objects, or difficult to find.

Over on the right is where you can see the properties of the currently selected object. You will be spending a lot of time in this area since it is where the functionality of each object on the dashboard is configured. For example when you want to map a graph to a piece of data or change the font or visibility on any part of the dashboard.

Right in the middle upper section of the screen, you can see the dashboard layout (or canvas) area, where you will be positioning your objects. One of the really nice features of Dashboards is that the components in this area refresh in real time based on data in the spreadsheet area below.

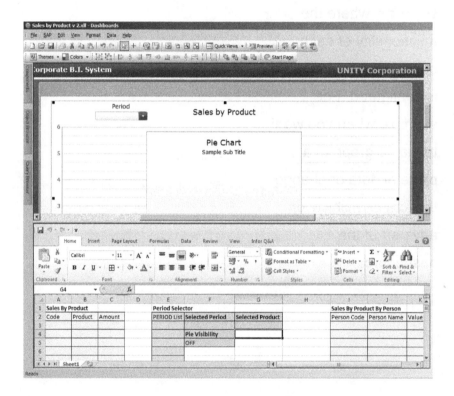

The lower central portion of the screen is the spreadsheet area, which is basically just an embedded Excel instance.

40

Any data sources write data into pre-defined areas of this spreadsheet and any dashboard objects read data from areas of the spreadsheet.

The really cool thing about this, is that you have virtually all of the native Excel functionality available to you to format data, concatenate values, perform calculations etc. So the data in your database can be enhanced in this area before being presented to the user.

Define a Spreadsheet Area

The first thing you need to do, is define an area of the spreadsheet where the data from the web service will be placed. We want to create 2 columns, one for the values and one for the product names associated with those values. So on the spreadsheet we colour an area, put a border around it and add headings for our columns. We know how many products there are, so we know how many rows will be returned from our query, so we highlight that many rows.

	A	B	C	D
1				
2		Product	Amount	
3		a	100	
4		b	150	
5		c	200	
6				
7				
8				
9				

We can even enter some sample data into the spreadsheet so that this will be immediately reflected in the components that we add later.

Connect to the Data Source

We need to connect our spreadsheet to the data source we created earlier, so that the data from the web service can be populated into the spreadsheet, in the area we have defined. To do this, select **Data / Connections** from the menu.

In the dialogue that appears select **Add / Web Service Connection** and enter a name for the new connection, something similar to the name of the query you created earlier would be good.

Next go back to FlyNet Data Connect and open up your web service, look for the link to the WSDL URL and click on it. This will put the link into the clipboard.

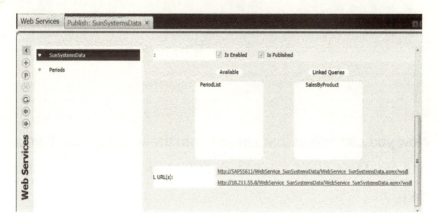

Paste it into the WSDL URL field and press the Import button

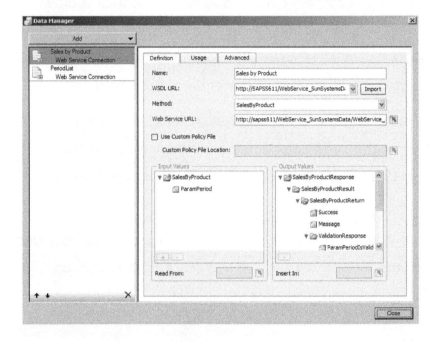

Now you can select the method from the web service. If you had created several queries, then they would all be available here.

Next, you will see that the response fields that will come back containing data from the database, via the web service, are contained in the Output Values section.

Select the first one that you wish to map to the spreadsheet, in my case Param_AMOUNT and press the **Insert In** lookup button.

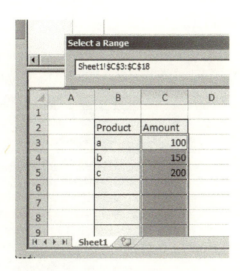

Highlight the range of cells where the data is to be placed and click OK on the range selector dialogue.

Repeat this for every column of data in the web service that you wish to map. Note that, if you want to map all the columns, then you can directly map the node which contains the individual columns to the spreadsheet and it will map all the columns within it.

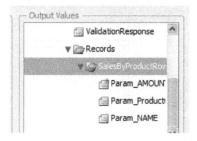

Next click on the Usage tab and ensure the Refresh Before Components Are Loaded check box is ticked. This will cause the data to be read from the web service into the Flash chart, as it is being displayed to the user.

Now you can close the data dialogue.

Adding a Chart

Now we need to add a way to display the data to the user. In this case our intention is to display a bar chart. So we hover over the Components tab on the far left and from the pane that pops out, we select the Column Chart object and click on the canvas to deposit it there.

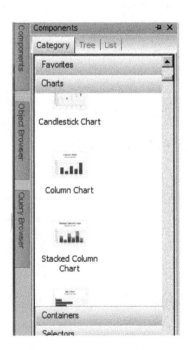

At this stage you can stretch it out to fill the desired space.

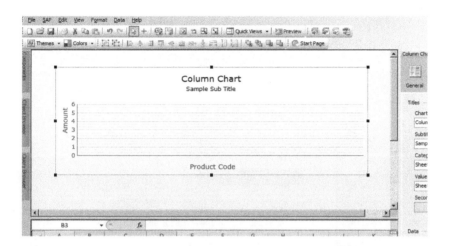

Next we need to tell the chart object where it can find the data.

Over on the right, in the data pane, click the **By Series** radio button and click the plus sign below the series window. Enter a new series called product.

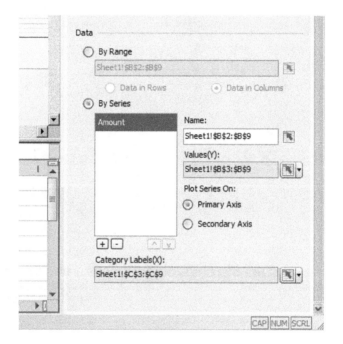

Next, click the Values (Y) lookup button and select the range of cells in the spreadsheet that encompass the values column. Do not select the column header.

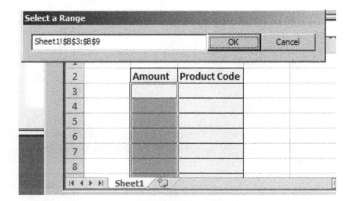

Next, do the same for the Category Labels(X).

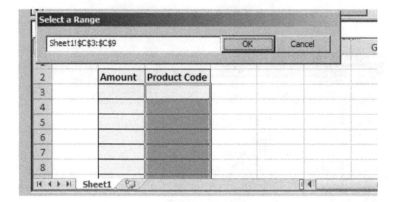

You should see the chart start to take shape right in front of you.

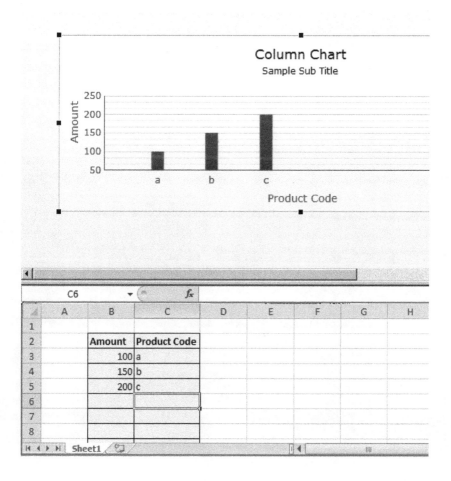

Now all that remains is to preview your chart with real data. Click on the preview button on the toolbar and Dashboards opens the preview window, fires the Data Connect web service, retrieves the data, places it into the spreadsheet in the place you reserved for it and displays the graph, based on that data.

Congratulations you have created your first data aware Flash control.

Filter By Accounting Period

Dashboards supports user interactivity, whereby the designer can display a control on the screen, that the viewer will use to affect the data that is displayed. In our example of sales by product, we are currently displaying all the data from our financial system, for all months and years. We are going to provide a filter for the user to allow them to select a particular period to show the data for.

In order to do this, the first thing we need to do is create a query that returns a list of all the accounting periods for which we have data. We also need to build a filter into our initial query, so that it only returns data for the specified period.

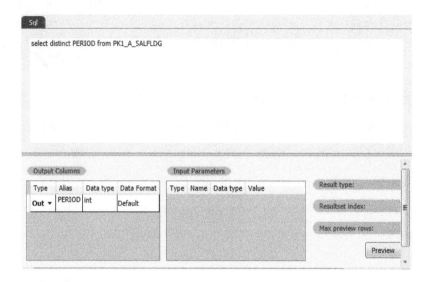

We add a new query to the DataConnect designer:

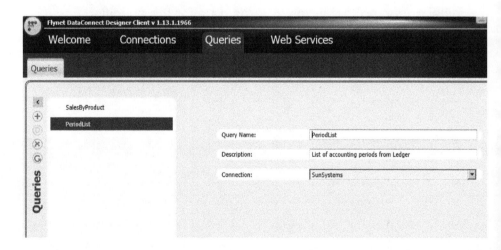

and publish it as a web service:

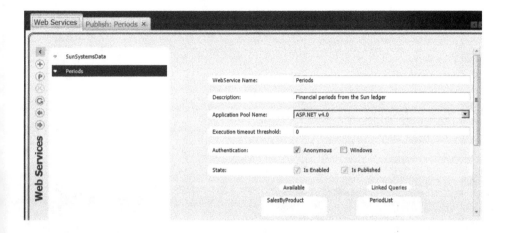

On testing we can see that it returns a list of all periods that are used in the ledger table:

Dashboards for Beginners

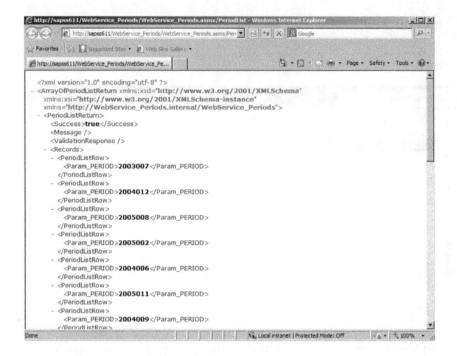

```xml
<?xml version="1.0" encoding="utf-8" ?>
<ArrayOfPeriodListReturn xmlns:xsd="http://www.w3.org/2001/XMLSchema"
  xmlns:xsi="http://www.w3.org/2001/XMLSchema-instance"
  xmlns="http://WebService_Periods.internal/WebService_Periods">
  <PeriodListReturn>
    <Success>true</Success>
    <Message />
    <ValidationResponse />
    <Records>
      <PeriodListRow>
        <Param_PERIOD>2003007</Param_PERIOD>
      </PeriodListRow>
      <PeriodListRow>
        <Param_PERIOD>2004012</Param_PERIOD>
      </PeriodListRow>
      <PeriodListRow>
        <Param_PERIOD>2005008</Param_PERIOD>
      </PeriodListRow>
      <PeriodListRow>
        <Param_PERIOD>2005002</Param_PERIOD>
      </PeriodListRow>
      <PeriodListRow>
        <Param_PERIOD>2004006</Param_PERIOD>
      </PeriodListRow>
      <PeriodListRow>
        <Param_PERIOD>2005011</Param_PERIOD>
      </PeriodListRow>
      <PeriodListRow>
        <Param_PERIOD>2004009</Param_PERIOD>
      </PeriodListRow>
```

Next we need to set an area of the spreadsheet to where we can return the list of periods to. As before we set a background colour and a heading.

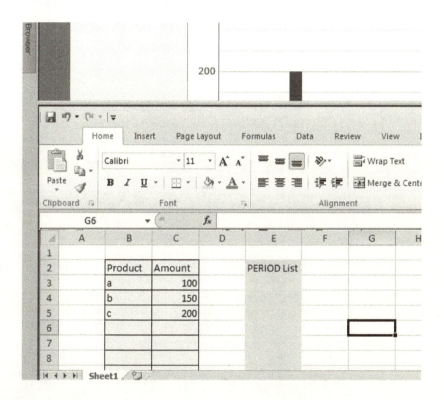

As before, we pick up the WSDL URL from DataConnect and create a data connection in Dashboards based around it. Again, this one is set to refresh before load.

WSDL URL(s): http://SAPSS611/WebService_Periods/WebService_Periods.asmx?wsdl
http://10.211.55.8/WebService_Periods/WebService_Periods.asmx?wsdl

Adding the Selector

There are a number of selectors available but we are going to use a simple single value selector on this occasion.

From the Selectors section of the components palette, we pick the Combo box and drag it right onto the canvas. Note that we can even position it on top of our chart object!

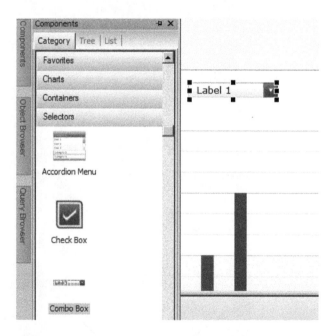

If you need to position objects on top of other objects then you can use the various arrangement tools to move items from back to front on the toolbar.

Next we set a title for the combo box and tell it to get its labels from the rage on the spreadsheet that we defined previously.

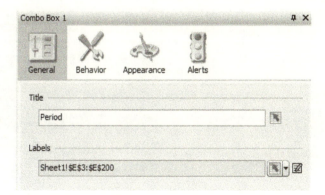

Then we select cell F3 as the destination for the selected value. Note we have also provided a heading and colour for that cell.

Now we need to modify our original query to accept the period parameter. We achieve this by modifying the SQL as follows:

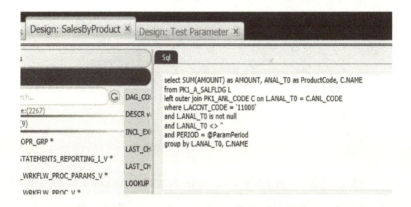

Notice how we can choose any name for the parameter, in this example ParamPeriod and simply prefix it with an @ symbol to indicate that it is a parameter.

Now when we publish and test the web service, we are asked to enter our parameter value:

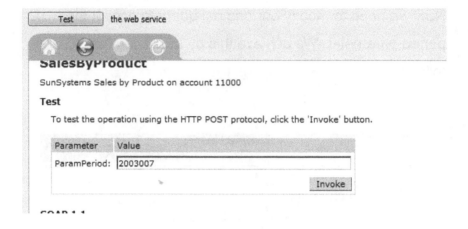

Next we need to modify the data source in Dashboards to accept the parameter value from the result of what the user selected. Remember this is going to go into cell F3.

We must edit the data connection and start by re-importing it. Once we have done this we can see that the ParamPeriod value is available to use in the Input Values pane.

We map this to cell F3

Finally we change the usage to refresh on trigger by mapping the trigger cell to F3 and leaving the default "when the value changes" selected.

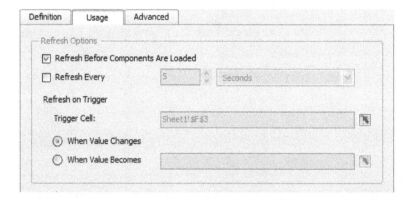

Now when we preview the dashboard, we can select a value from the drop down and see the graph refresh to reflect our selection.

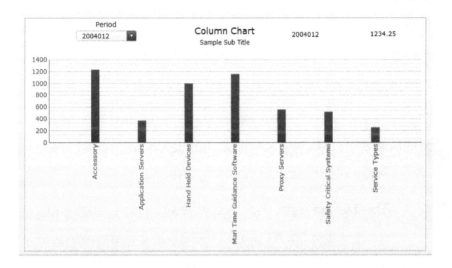

Debugging your Dashboard

If you are paying attention you may have noticed that on my chart above there are two pieces of data visible at the top right. One saying 2004012 and one saying 1234.25. These are labels that I have used to monitor what is going on inside the spreadsheet while previewing the dashboard.

The problem is that when we execute (preview) the dashboard, there are a lot of actions taking place. In this simple example the following things happen:

1. The Period data source queries the database and returns a list of all period values to the spreadsheet

2. The period values are read from the spreadsheet and displayed in a list for the user to select from

3. When the user makes a selection the selected value is placed in a cell on the spreadsheet.

4. This change of data triggers the SalesByProduct query to execute

5. The SalesByProduct query reads the parameter value from the spreadsheet and fetches the data from its data source

70

6. The data coming back from the database is written to the spreadsheet

7. The graph updates reading the refreshed spreadsheet data.

With all this activity going on, if something isn't quite working correctly, it is important to be able to easily diagnose where the problem has occurred. This can be achieve simply and effectively by placing labels on the dashboard that reflect data from the spreadsheet and the data sources.

In my example, I wanted to know that when the user makes a selection from the list of periods, that it was in fact being written to the prescribed cell on the spreadsheet. So I placed a label control (which is available under the text components) onto the dashboard.

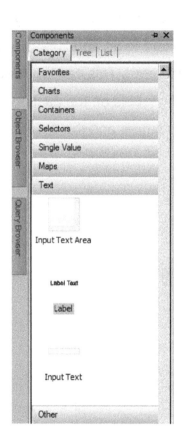

I then mapped the label control to the cell where the user selected value should have been returned to.

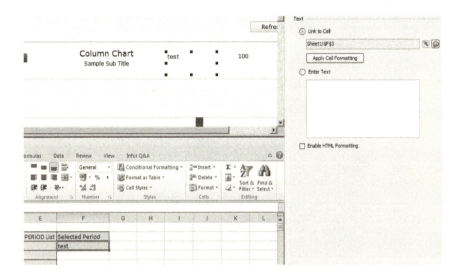

Here you can see the label selected, the mapping over on the right and the Selected Period cell in the spreadsheet below. Notice that I have typed a value into the cell so that I can see instantly that my label is reflecting that value.

I did the same thing with the first value of the amount column that is returned from the SalesByProduct data set.

Dashboards for Beginners

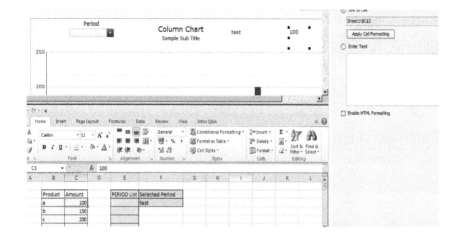

Finally, I mapped the Success and Messages values from the data connection to a couple of cells on the spreadsheet.

With these messages and internal values mapped to labels on my dashboard I was able to see exactly how far through the process the system had got and what values were being returned, so it made it very easy to debug the build.

Another useful thing to do, is force a manual refresh of the chart data. Currently our chart is designed to refresh when the user selects a value from the list of periods. If for some reason this refresh doesn't work, then it could be because one of the data connections is not returning values or maybe because the refresh mechanism itself has a problem. To eliminate one of these possibilities, we can add a manual refresh button to the chart. This is over in the components palette under Web Connectivity.

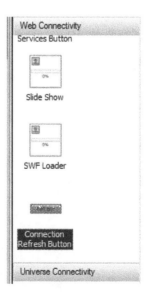

Under the properties of the refresh button you can select which connections are refreshed.

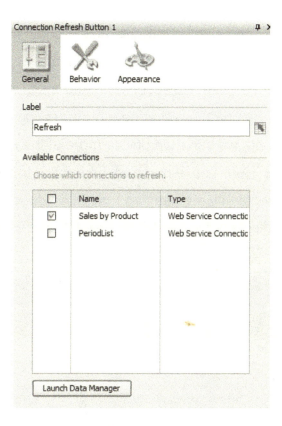

Dynamic Chart Titles

With the chart selected, under the General section over on the right, we can see the chart title and subtitle. It is possible to simply enter text into these fields and they will appear as fixed text on the chart. However, as in our example, when the basis of the chart can change e.g. displaying data for a different period, we can map one or more of the titles to the spreadsheet. Here I have mapped the subtitle to the period that was selected by the user, so now when the chart executes it displays the period number for which it is running.

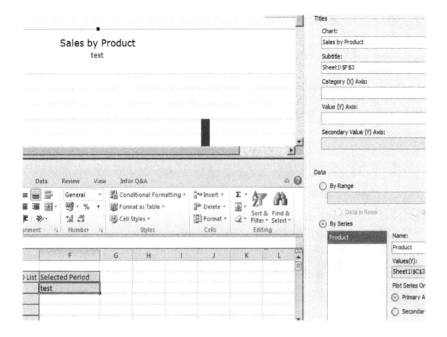

Spread it around

Notice on this version of the chart, the bars all seem to be gathering as if for a secret discussion, over on the left hand side.

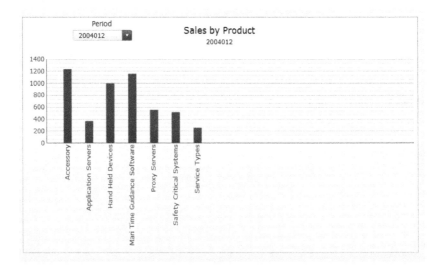

This is likely to occur of course, because we have a variable number of products that could appear in our list for any given period that the user selects. So to counteract this and spread the bars evenly across the chart, regardless of how many products are represented, we need to look at the behaviour section of the chart properties and enable the check boxes under "ignore blank cells". That way, only cells with data will be returned to the chart object and the bars will be spread evenly.

Pop Up Drill Downs

I remember a time before the world had ever heard of anything called a drill in computer software terms. Of course dentists have always had them and you will be pleased to know that drilling is a lot less painful in Business Objects Dashboards! In fact we are going to do something quite cool now, where we will enable to user to click on any of the bars of the bar chart, to select one of the products and then pop open a pie chart, right over the top of the bar chart, showing the breakdown of which sales people were responsible for the sales represented by that particular bar.

Initially when we created the chart, we only brought back the sales person names, because that's all we wanted to show on our chart. Well, now we need the product code too, because what we are aiming to do here is create another query which filters the data a bit further.

You will recall that our current query to create the chart, selects sales value for a particular account code, in a user defined accounting period and then groups the value by the product code, effectively giving us a total sales value for each product in a period.

The next query will have to do exactly the same, but for a single product and then grouped by sales person.

So if this is our data set:

	Period 2012/08
Products	Sales Value
Product 1	100
Product 2	150
Product 3	200

What we want to do is drill into one of the values, let's say Product 2 and see how much of that value is attributable to each sales person.

	Period 2012/08
Products	Sales Value
Product 1	100
Product 2	150
Product 3	200

Sales Person	Value
Bob Smith	50
Sarah Jones	100

So firstly we amend our original data set, to write the product code column to the spreadsheet.

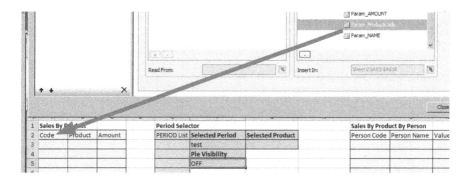

Next we need to allow insertion from the chart, so that when the user clicks on one of the bars, the data from that bar is inserted into a cell in the spreadsheet. Naturally we create an area on the spreadsheet, called Selected Product to accept the value.

With the chart component selected we use the row type insertion style. If you click on the little speech bubble to the right of the insertion type, you will see a short animated video of how it works and what different types are available.

Next select the product series and tell it to get its source data from the list of product codes which are returned by the SalesByProduct query and tell it to place the result in the new Selected Product cell.

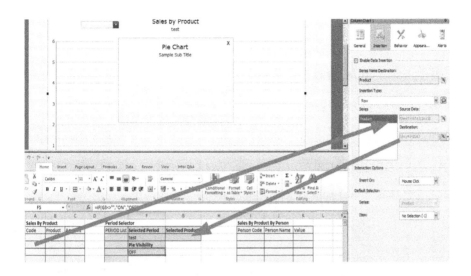

Next we need a query to return our sales by product by sales person, this is what my example query looked like:

select sum(AMOUNT), ANAL_T3, NAME from PK1_A_SALFLDG L

LEFT OUTER JOIN PK1_ANL_CODE AN on AN.ANL_CODE = L.ANAL_T3 and ANL_CAT_ID = '14'

where L.ANAL_T0 = @ProductCode

and L.PERIOD = @Period

and L.ACCNT_CODE = '11000'

Group by L.ANAL_T3, NAME

In my case ANAL_T3 is the sales person analysis code from my financial ledger and I get the description of that code from the joined table PK1_ANL_CODE. The parameters @ProductCode and @Period are used to filter the data based on user selection.

Now we need to make this query run based on the data from our spreadsheet parameters, so we publish it as a data source and then place it into the data manager.

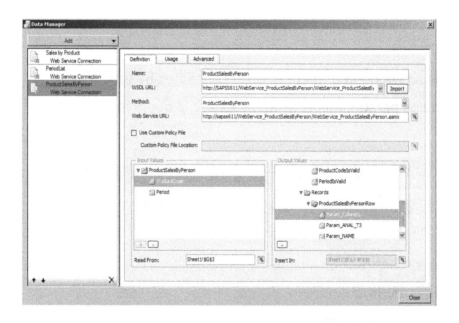

Notice how the two input parameters are fed from the cells on the spreadsheet where the original accounting period is from when we used it before for the drop down selector and the newly created Product Code cell.

F	G
:ctor	
Selected Period	Selected Product
test	

The result goes to a new area on our spreadsheet.

Person Code	Person Name	Value

Next we need to add a pie chart object to the dashboard and link its data to the results from our new query.

This is simply a matter of dropping the pie chart onto the canvas and modifying the properties in the now familiar manner.

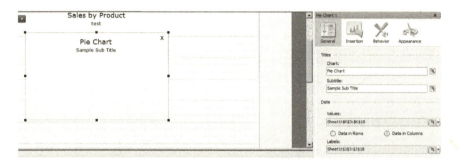

Now if we were to run our dashboard we would see the pie chart appearing over the top of the bar chart, which is fine, but we only want it to appear when a user has selected one of the bars. To achieve this we need to use the visibility property to switch the pie chart on and off. Visibility is controlled by a value in a cell, so for example you can select a cell and have the pie chart visible when the value in the cell is "ON" and invisible when the value in the cell is "OFF".

I selected a cell as follows:

		=IF(G3<>"","ON","OFF")	
D	E	F	G
	Period Selector		
	PERIOD List	Selected Period	Selected Product
		test	
		Pie Visibility	
		OFF	

I added a formula into this cell, to populate it with the word ON if G3 (the selected product) was not blank, i.e. if the user has selected a product then the visibility trigger will read ON and then OFF under any other condition.

Next, in the pie chart behaviour properties, we set the Dynamic Visibility status to point at the cell where the on or off value will be and set the key to ON. That means that when the value in the status cell is the same as the value we put in the key cell, the visibility will be set to ON.

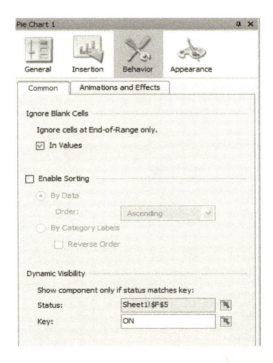

Finally, we need to give the user a way of switching off the visibility, so they can get back to clicking on the chart to select other products to examine.

To do this, I used a push button component from the selectors section of the components gallery.

To provide a familiar look and feel, I dragged the push button to a small square, made the label value a bold capital X and placed the push button in the top right hand corner of the pie chart area. The button was set to source data from a blank cell on the spreadsheet and place it into the selected product cell, which you will remember controls the visibility of the pie chart. So by placing a blank value into that cell, we cause the pie visibility cell to switch to OFF and hence the pie chart vanishes.

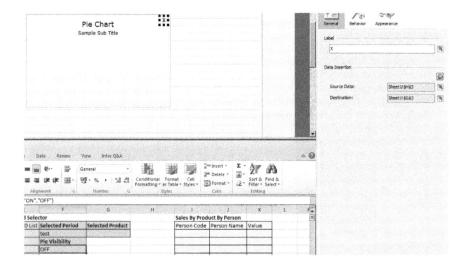

Finally, I linked the visibility of the push button to the same visibility cell and criteria as the pie chart so that it would become visible and invisible along with the pie chart.

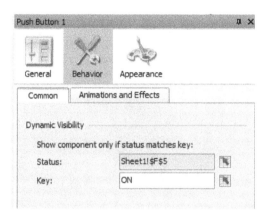

Now, whenever the user clicks on a bar in the chart, the pie chart appears, showing the breakdown of the bar between sales people and it vanishes again when the user clicks the x in the top right.

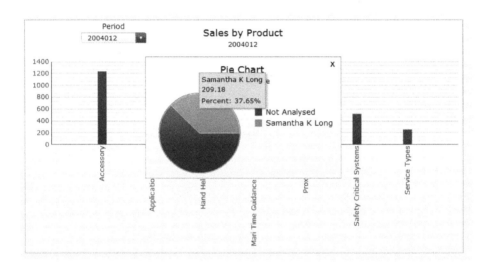

An alternative to using an "X" in the top right corner is to put no text at all in the button and stretch it out over the entire pie chart, or even over the entire bar chart. That way the user could click anywhere on the pie chart, or even anywhere on the bar chart to close the pie. Try out a few different methods and see which works best for your user community.

Notice also, how there is built in functionality to display data about the underlying object when the mouse hovers over it. You will be pleased to know that this happens automatically and you don't need to do any coding to make it occur!

Adding some Style

There's not much point having a fancy graphical BI solution, if you just go and use plain backgrounds and don't bother branding the result with your corporate identity, so impress the boss and take a look at the ways you can make your dashboards look pretty!

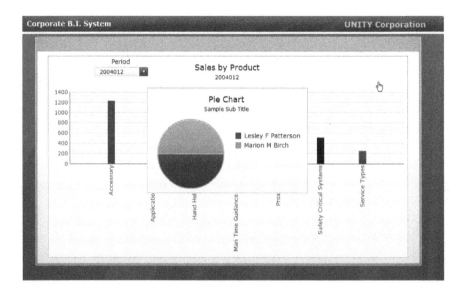

I used some very simple to implement components to modify my dashboard to look like the above screenshot. Again, over on the left, in the components palette, you will find the backgrounds, containers, image objects and labels that can be used to dress up your dashboard. These are all pretty much self explanatory, so take the time to experiment and see what you can achieve.

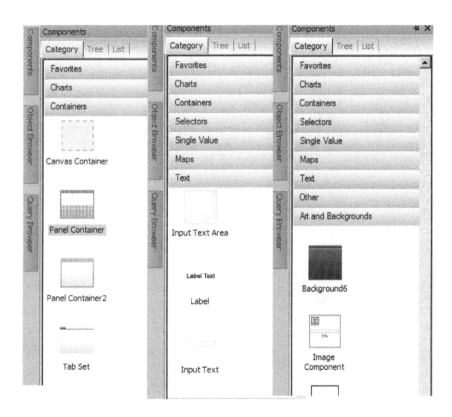

Components

Column Chart Range Finder

We have been using the column chart and pie chart throughout this guide so far. Just before we leave this most versatile control, there is one more rather cute aspect to be discovered – the Range Slider. You will find it as a check box over on the common behaviour properties pannel. Enable it and you will see that it allows the user to reduce the number of columns on the chart simply by sliding each end of the range finder line in towards the centre.

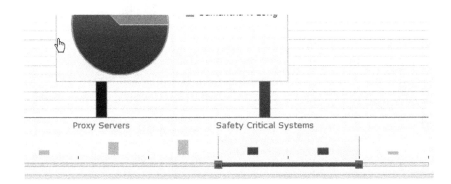

Tab Control

The tab control is very useful for adding a large number of items to a dashboard and allowing the user to swap between pages of dashboard items. It can be found under the **Containers** section. To add or remove a tab, use the +/- buttons that appear when Tab 1 is selected. Note, to move the tab control you need to click on the actual tabs and drag those.

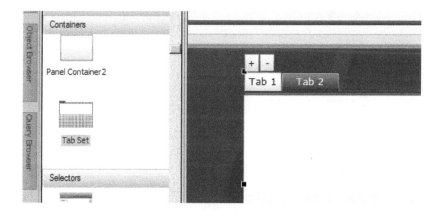

Placing other components on the tab control is simply a matter of dragging them into place.

OHLC and Candlestick

OHLC stands for Open High Low Close and is often used for stock prices, to show the opening price, the all time high and low and finally the closing price. It could equally be used in finance systems to show sales performance by sales people or product, against budget, over a time duration. The best way to understand these controls is to create a section of your spreadsheet containing rows for opening, high, low and closing data as follows:

B	C	D	E	F
Stock Name	Stock1	Stock 2	Stock 3	Stock 4
Open	100	150	125	95
High	300	175	150	190
Low	50	60	70	20
Close	120	120	80	120

Then you can map the OHLC chart to it by mapping each of the OHLC series to the rows of the spreadsheet as shows below:

The result is that the verticle lines on the chart show the high and low values and the horizontal lines show the opening and closing values.

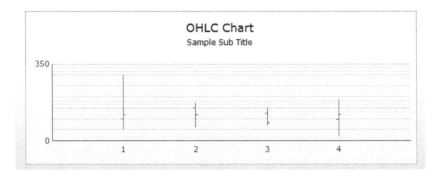

List Builder

Imagine if we had a lot of different stocks in our database. We might want to give the user the option to easily pick just a few of them to compare. This is a good use for the List Builder control, which allows us to pick values from our table and add them individually or in groups to the chart. In this screenshot we can see that we are comparing Stock 1 and 3 side by side.

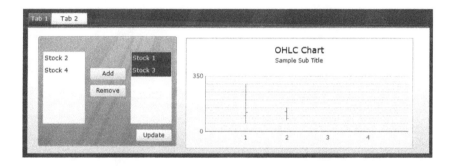

To achieve this, we need to bring the list builder onto the canvass, I have chosen to place it next to the chart. Then in the spreadsheet we need to set up an area to accept the data that the user will select in the list builder.

105

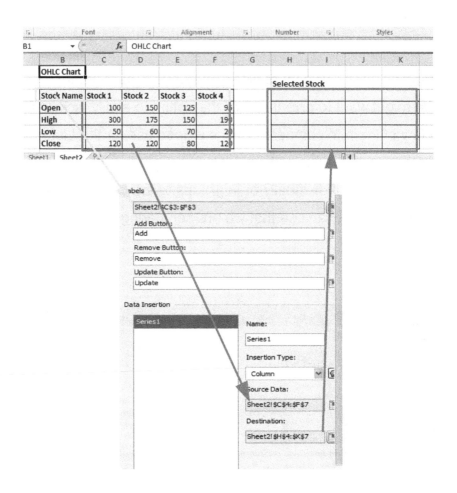

Now we configure the List Builder to read its labels (the values in the list to select from) from the stock names in the top row of the left hand part of the spreadsheet.

And we tell it to put the source data (which is picked up from the entire left hand data grid, into the right hand data grid.

Bubble Chart

The bubble chart is a very powerful type of chart as it allows you to plot data, not only on an x and y coordinate, but also to indicate another value in the size of the plot point. In the example below we can see that three products are represented, showing the sales value, the marketing spend that was used to achieve that sales value and the size of the plot point (or bubble) indicates the amount of profit. From this kind of chart we can easily see which items are the most profitable and where our marketing budget should be targetted.

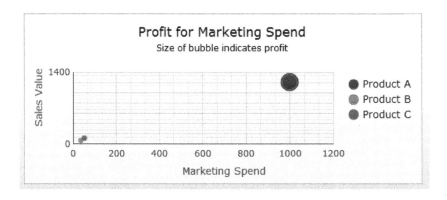

I used the following dataset to create this chart

	A1	▼	*fx*			
	A	B	C	D	E	F
1						
2	2012	Cost of Sales	Marketing Spend	Total Cost of Sales	Sales Value	Profit
3	Product A	100	1000	1100	1210	110
4	Product B	20	35	55	63.25	8.25
5	Product C	50	50	100	110	10
6						

then I mapped the bubble chart component to it as follows

Here we can see that each product on the chart has an X, Y and Size mapping and these are mapped to the appropriate field on the appropriate product line. In my example the X values are mapped to the marketing spend, the Y values are mapped to the sales value and the size is mapped to the profit.

Text Input

With this type of graph it would be great to allow the user to perform some what if analysis. So for example, they could try different values for the marketing spend and see how this affects overall profitability. It is possible to allow the user to input values in free text (i.e. without having to select them from a predefined list) by using the text input component, which can be found in the Text section.

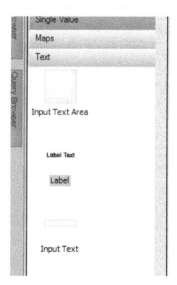

In my example I created 3 of these fields, labelled them and linked them to my Marketing Spend fields for each product on the spreadsheet.

Marketing Spend What if Analysis	
Product A:	1000
Product B:	35
Product C:	50

When mapping the component the linked cell is where the initial data value comes from when the component loads (so thats what the user gets to see) and the data insertion is where the user entered data is written to. You could equally use the Enter Text option instead of the Link to Cell to provide a starting value such as "Please enter a value".

I placed the What If entry group of fields next to the chart:

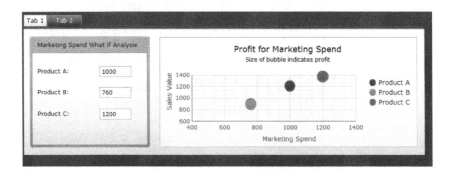

As soon as the user updates one of the fields, the chart instantly updates to reflect the effect of the new marketing budget!

Bubble charts can be very effective showing the movement of data over time. For some inspiration in this area, search TED (www.TED.com) for presentations by Hans Rosling.

Luckily we have the capability of presenting similar playbacks with all of our chart types, using the Play Selector.

The Spreadsheet Table

To demonstrate the play selector, we will actually use another selector (which can also be used as a display item) – the Spreadsheet Table. This is a simple little component which allows us to show raw spreadsheet data on our dashboard. Useful in its own right as a capture and display control, we are going to use it here to show what is really going on at the spreadsheet level when the play control is running.

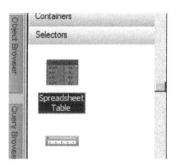

Start by copying the data grid from the previous example to a new spreadsheet tab as follows:

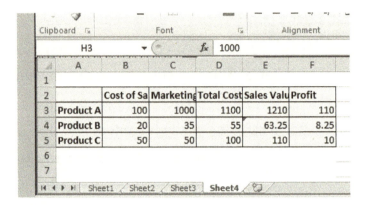

	A	B	C	D	E	F
1						
2		Cost of Sa	Marketing	Total Cost	Sales Valu	Profit
3	Product A	100	1000	1100	1210	110
4	Product B	20	35	55	63.25	8.25
5	Product C	50	50	100	110	10
6						
7						

Sheet1 / Sheet2 / Sheet3 / **Sheet4**

Next apply the spreadsheet table control to the canvass.

Tab 1	Tab 2	Tab 3				
	Cost of Sa	Marketin	Total Cos	Sales Valu	Profit
Product A	100	1000	1100	1210	110
Product B	20	35	55	63.25	8.25
Product C	50	50	100	110	10

I have chosen to apply it to a new tab on my tab control.

Next map it to the data area

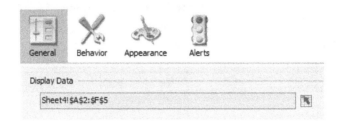

And you should be able to see the data from the spreadsheet, reflected in the control.

Naturally, you could enable the data insertion functionality of the control to allow the user to enter and modify data in the underlying data model too.

The Play Selector

Now, for our example, we are going to see what happens as marketing spend data changes over time. Of course you could use it to demonstrate any type of data change over time. The spreadsheet model we have bases its total sales and profitability figures on the marketing spend based on a simplified statistical model.

In order to get our marketing spend to change over time, we need to give the spreadsheet the marketing values, for each product, over a range of years. So we create a table like this:

G	H	I	J	K	L	M	
	Annual Marketing Budget						
	2007	2008	2009	2010	2011	2012	
	1000	500	1200	1500	900	500	
	35	70	200	300	400	500	
	50	75	900	700	400	200	

Now what we want is for the play control, so take each years marketing spend and swap it into the primary table, replacing the figures in the marketing spend column, one year at a time.

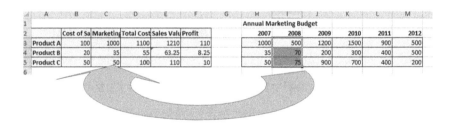

This means that the source data for the Play Selector is the whole of the Annual Marketing Budget table from H1 to M5 and the destination is the marketing Spend on the first table, column C.

Now when we preview our chart, we can see that the data in the Marketing Spend column changes as the play control runs.

Now if we swap out our display of the spreadsheet contents with the bubble chart from the previous example, we have a nice bubble chart that shows the change of data over time.

In my example, I have chosen to show both the chart and the underlying data for demonstration purposes.

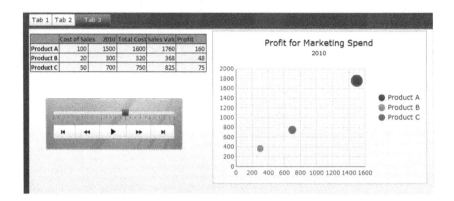

Finally, if you include the column headings from the source table in the play selectors source data and destination data, then the marketing column heading will change to reflect the year that is being displayed. You can map this to the sub heading of the chart and then the user get to see the year change as the data changes. Very effective!

Sliders, Dials, Gauges, Line Charts and Alerts

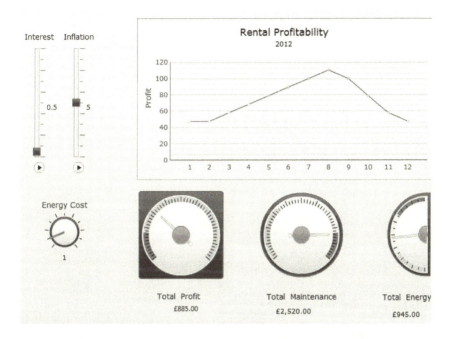

OK by now you are probably getting the hang of how most of these controls work so for our next example, we are going to create a dashboard for a fictional property rental company, This will demonstrate how we can create relatively complex spreadsheet data models, with built in logic and and analytics, then present it to the user in a very simple manner, whilst at the same time providing lots of interactivity. We will be using the line chart as our primary display mechanism along with different types of gauges and some controls in the form of sliders and dials.

First though we need to create our spreadsheet model for the fictional business.

The spreadsheet is divided into two sections, at the top we focus on standard and variable data and at the bottom we have the operational figures for the business by month – one line of the lower portion is where the chart will pull its data from. I would suggest that the easiest way to explore this example is to open the example file that can be downloaded from the readers section of my web site (see the Companion Web Site section for details)

	A	B	C	D	E	F	G	H	I	J	K	L	M	N	O
1	Variables		Base Costs												
2	Interest Rate	0.5	Rental Incom	1200		Monthly Repayment	833.3333		Maintenance Cost		200				
3	Inflation	5	Maintenance	200		Monthly Interest	4.166667		x Inflation		10				
4			Capital Loan	250000		Total Monthly Repay	837.5		Total Maintenance c		210				
5	Engy Multiple	1	Loan Term	300											
6	Energy	100	100	90	80	70	60	50	40	50	70	90	100		
7		Jan	Feb	Mar	Apr	May	Jun	Jul	Aug	Sep	Oct	Nov	Dec		
8	Rental Income	1200	1200	1200	1200	1200	1200	1200	1200	1200	1200	1200	1200		
9	Mortgage	837.5	837.5	837.5	837.5	837.5	837.5	837.5	837.5	837.5	837.5	837.5	837.5		
10	Maintenance	210	210	210	210	210	210	210	210	210	210	210	210	£2,520.00	Total Annual Maintenance
11	Energy	105	105	94.5	84	73.5	63	52.5	42	52.5	73.5	94.5	105	£945.00	Total Annual Energy
12	Profit	47.5	47.5	58	68.5	79	89.5	100	110.5	100	79	58	47.5	£885.00	Total Annual Profit
13	Total Cost	1152.5	1152.5	1142	1131.5	1121	1110.5	1100	1089.5	1100	1121	1142	1152.5	£13,515.00	Total Annual Cost
14	Total Income	1200	1200	1200	1200	1200	1200	1200	1200	1200	1200	1200	1200		
15		Jan	Feb	Mar	Apr	May	Jun	Jul	Aug	Sep	Oct	Nov	Dec		

Understanding the model

First we have the variables section

Variables	
Interest Rate	0.5
Inflation	5
Engy Multiplie	1
Energy	100

This is where we specify the interest rate, the inflation rate and the energy multiple. Each of these items is linked to a control dial of some description, which allows the user to tweak the values.

Next we have the base costs, rental income which is fixed to 1200 per month, maintenance which is budgeted at 200 per month, the capital loan (or mortgage) and the term of the loan. The loan information and the interest rate are used to calculate the total monthly repayment on the mortgage using spreadsheet formulas. Finally we have an assumed rate of inflation applied to the maintenance cost.

Base Costs						
Rental Incom	1200		Monthly Repayment	833.3333	Maintenance Cost	200
Maintenance	200		Monthly Interest	4.166667	x Inflation	10
Capital Loan	250000		Total Monthly Repay	837.5	Total Maintenance c	210
Loan Term	300					

In the lower portion of the spreadsheet we we use the base figures from above to lay out our monthly costs, resulting in a total profit calculation.

7		Jan	Feb	Mar	Apr
8	Rental Income	1200	1200	1200	1200
9	Mortgage	837.5	837.5	837.5	837.5
10	Maintenance	210	210	210	210
11	Energy	105	105	94.5	84
12	Profit	47.5	47.5	58	68.5
13	Total Cost	1152.5	1152.5	1142	1131.5
14	Total Income	1200	1200	1200	1200

Then over on the right we sum up some of the lines for use in our gauges.

	L	M	N	O	P	Q
	200					
	10					
c	210					
)	90	100				
	Nov	Dec				
)	1200	1200				
5	837.5	837.5				
)	210	210	£2,520.00	Total Annual Maintenance		
5	94.5	105	£945.00	Total Annual Energy		
)	58	47.5	£885.00	Total Annual Profit		
L	1142	1152.5	£13,515.00	Total Annual Cost		
)	1200	1200				

Naturally you can create your own model to base these dashboards on and of course you can source the data from a database if you prefer.

The Line Chart

Drag a line chart out onto the canvass and map it to the Profit line on the spreadsheet. Then map the monthly column headings to the category labels.

This gives us our basic line chart. We can tidy it up a bit by modifying the appearance aspects.

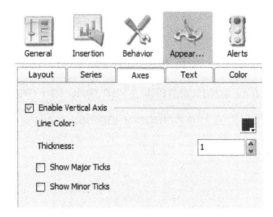

Finally we can add some alerts. Note that for this type of component the alerts are only available if there is a single series of data. In my example I set the alerts to work on a value, then typed 3 ranges of values into the coloured grid below, finally checking the box that indicates that high values are good.

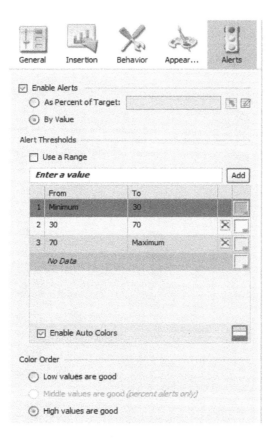

This is enough information for the chart component to display our profit data, showing small coloured dots for the value points and changing the colour of those according to the alert status. So for example if the value is between 0 and 30, then the dot goes red.

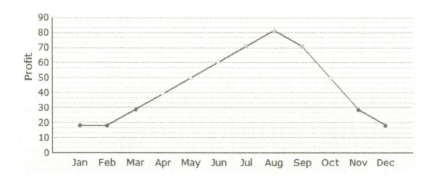

Sliders

In my example I have used two sliders for the interest rate and inflation.

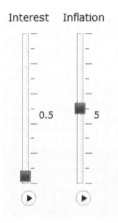

These are linked to the variables section of the spreadsheet:

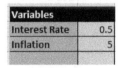

With a very simple single cell mapping. Finally we specify the scale, from 0 to 10, so that when the user slides the slider the value it inserts to the spreadsheet will be from 0 to 10.

On the behaviour tab there is also a check box to enable the play button and set the time for the playback. This allows sliders to be used to control animated charts.

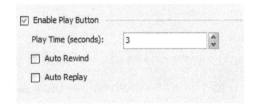

Dials

The dial controls work in exactly the same way as the sliders, in my case I mapped one to the Energy cost multiplier cell.

Gauges

Dials and gauges are standard fare for dashboards so you will find a number of different types of each in the pallette. I have added three different styles to my example, so a) you can see the difference and b) you can see how terrible it looks to use different styles on the same dashboard!

Despite their different appearance, they all work in the same manner. Start by dragging a gauge control onto the canvass.

I have mapped mine to the single value line totals over in column N of my spreadsheet.

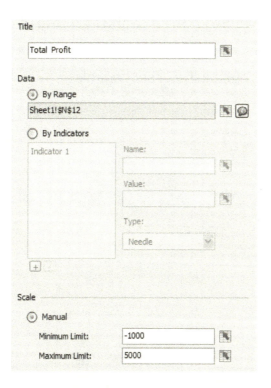

And set a manual scale, i.e. the minimum and maximum values on the dial, so that the needle will hover somewhere in between. Obviously to do this you need to know the possible range of values that the needle could travel to, dependent on the variable inputs. If you don't then there are a number of automatic methods to select from too.

You can select which values are shown, in the appearance section, the font and position of the label can also be chosen, with the ability to move the label further away from the host object using the offset controls.

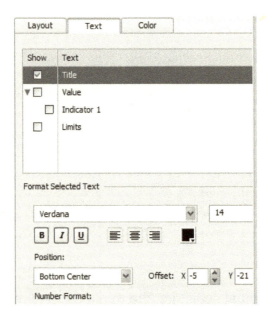

Alerts really come into their own on a gauge control, enable the alerts and play around with the various options, I have chosen to use the percentage of target in my example and enter into the coloured grid the percentage values. So if the value is between 0 and 30% (indicating profits are low) then it is seen as bad and if it is between 70% and the maximum then it is indicating a high profit and seen as good, thus pushing the needle into the green zone. I have set this by selecting High Values are Good.

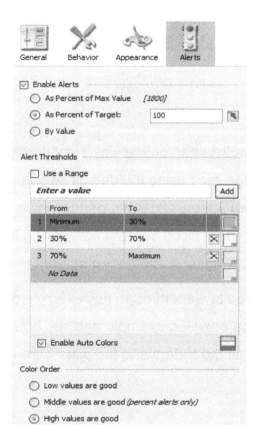

Total Profit
£885.00

Personally I wasn't keen on the way the value was displayed within the gauge itself using the default setting, so I switched it off and placed a label under the gauge which was linked directly to the same value cell that was driving the gauge, thus providing a digital readout for purposes of accuracy.

I encourage you to work through this example or have a play around with the provided example and see how it responds when you tweak the sliders and the dial.

Scorecards

Scorecards are typically used to provide data about performance against a pre-defined metric, for example sales or expenditure against budget, Sales person performance against target or machine operating temperatures against allowable limits. Each of the items you are measuring can show a set of current values, the comparison values and a graphic to indicate if the measurement is on track, below or exceeding the target.

Category	Q1	Q2		YTD Cost	YTD Budget
Office Rental	3000	⇒	3000	6000	6000
Equipment Rental	1000	↗	1200	2200	2000
Marketing	1500	↗	2000	3500	4000
Legal Fees	950	↘	200	1150	500
Electricity	650	↗	700	1350	1200
Communications	850	↗	1000	1850	2000
Fuel	1500	↘	1000	2500	2000

For our example we are going to show Quarter 1 and Quarter 2 expenditure against budget, for a range of expenditure items, like Office Rental and Electricity.

We will show an icon on the Q2 figure to indicate if the cost is below (downward pointing green arrow), above (upward pointing red arrow) or the same as (level amber arrow), the figure from Q1.

Against the Year to Date (YTD) cost we will show an icon indicating where the cost is in terms of the budget.

If the cost is between zero and 90% of the budget, i.e. we still have plenty of budget to play with, then we will show a green tick. If the cost is with between 90% to 110% then we will show an amber exclamation, because now our cost is approaching or slightly exceeding budget. Finally, if we are more that 110% over budget we will show a red cross.

In the budget column we will highlight the background of any budget that has been exceeded, with a bright red colour.

So to start we need to create a spreadsheet showing our expenditure and budget columns as follows:

	A	B	C	D	E
2					
3	Category	Q1	Q2	YTD Cost	YTD Budget
4	Office Rental	3000	3000	6000	6000
5	Equipment Rental	1000	1200	2200	2000
6	Marketing	1500	2000	3500	4000
7	Legal Fees	950	200	1150	500
8	Electricity	650	700	1350	1200
9	Communications	850	1000	1850	2000
10	Fuel	1500	1000	2500	2000
11					

The YTD Cost is a sum of the Q1 and Q2 budget row and the YTD Budget is simply and entered value. Of course these could all be provided by a database through DataConnect.

Next we need to drag a new scorecard component to the dashboard. This can be found in the Selectors section of the palette.

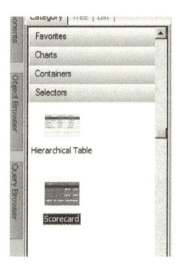

Now we need to map our scorecard to the spreadsheet. If the spreadsheet is neatly formatted then this is a very easy task. Use the Display Data selector and select the entire data range on the spreadsheet, including the column headings.

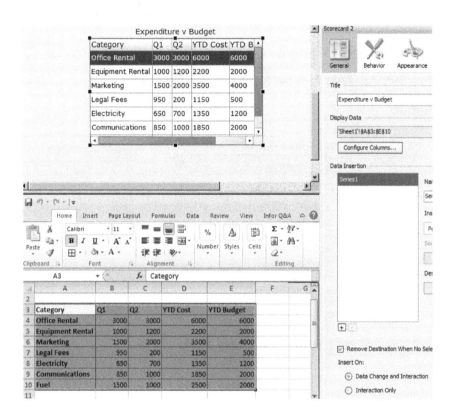

Notice that some of the column heading for YTD Budget is falling off the right hand edge of the Scorecard and the other columns are just about big enough to fit the headings and numbers. So stretch out the scorecard a bit and the press the **Configure Columns** button. Now you can set the column widths, bearing in mind that for the Q2, YTD Cost and YTD Budget, you will want to allow a little more space than is required for the values alone, because we will be putting the indicators in these fields too.

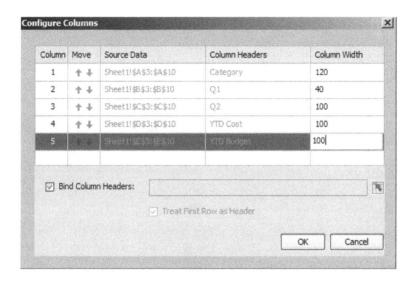

Notice at the bottom there is the possibility to bind the column headers to a different place in the spreadsheet, in case your spreadsheet is not as neatly defined as mine. Also you can ensure that the **Treat First Row as Header** check box is active, so that your spreadsheet column headings are used as the chart header. This should have your scorecard in reasonable shape and ready to accept the alert indicators.

Expenditure v Budget				
Category	Q1	Q2	YTD Cost	YTD Budget
Office Rental	3000	3000	6000	6000
Equipment Rental	1000	1200	2200	2000
Marketing	1500	2000	3500	4000
Legal Fees	950	200	1150	500
Electricity	650	700	1350	1200
Communications	850	1000	1850	2000
Fuel	1500	1000	2500	2000

Scorecard Alerts

The first alert we want to set is on the Q2 column, to indicate if it is higher, lower or the same as the previous quarter. Select the Alerts properties page and click the Q2 column check box.

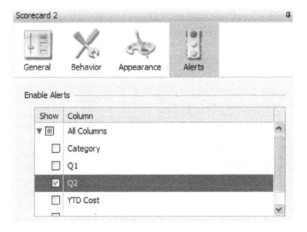

We are going to use the Percentage of Target mapping method, to compare our Q2 figures as a percentage of the Q1 figures. The **alert values** are the figures to be compared and the **As Percent of Target** figures are the figure against which we are comparing. So in this example I am mapping **Alert Values** to the Q2 column and the **As Percent of Target** to the Q1 column.

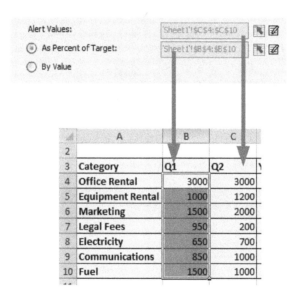

Now we need to set the alert thresholds. In our example, if the Q2 budget is between the minimum and 99% of the Q2 budget we are going to consider that it has reduced. So initially, in the **To** column of the **Alert Thresholds** dialogue, enter 99%.

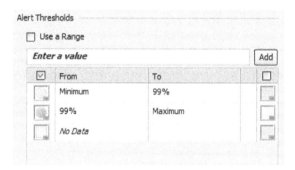

Next click on the **Enable Auto Colours** check box, to DISABLE it.

Now you can click on the green circle next to the Minimum

row of the **Alert Thresholds**

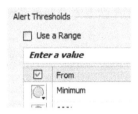

This allows you to set the icon shape and colour, for the icon

that will appear when Q2 is LOWER than Q1, so this will be

a green downward pointing arrow.

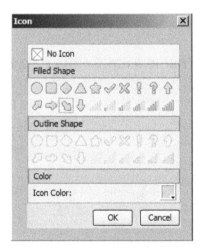

You should see that your preview is instantly updated to show the indicators in the correct rows.

Expenditure v Budget				
Category	Q1	Q2	YTD Cost	YTD Budget
Office Rental	3000	● 3000	6000	6000
Equipment Rental	1000	● 1200	2200	2000
Marketing	1500	● 2000	3500	4000
Legal Fees	950	⚘ 200	1150	500
Electricity	650	● 700	1350	1200
Communications	850	● 1000	1850	2000
Fuel	1500	⚘ 1000	2500	2000

When you entered 99% earlier in the **Alert Thresholds** it caused the first alert to clash with the second alert, which started at 30% and finished at 70%, so the second alert was deleted. We need to add it in again, so type 101% in the **Add** box and click the **Add** button.

Don't worry if you make a mistake, you can always hit the red X to delete the row. Now click on the icon for the 99%-101% line and set it to an amber, horizontal arrow:

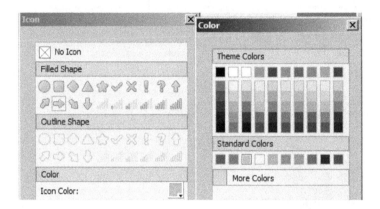

Click the Icon Colour square to access the colour editor.

Finally set the 101% to Maximum to a red, upward pointing arrow:

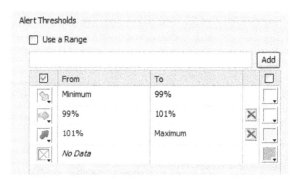

Again you should see the chart update in real time to show your new icons.

Category	Q1	Q2		YTD Cost	YTD Budget
Office Rental	3000	⇒	3000	6000	6000
Equipment Rental	1000	⬈	1200	2200	2000
Marketing	1500	⬈	2000	3500	4000
Legal Fees	950	⬊	200	1150	500
Electricity	650	⬈	700	1350	1200
Communications	850	⬈	1000	1850	2000
Fuel	1500	⬊	1000	2500	2000

Expenditure v Budget

Next we need to add the exclamations, ticks and crosses to the YTD Cost column. As before, check the column for which you want to apply the alerts.

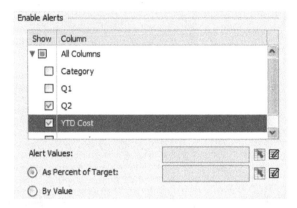

Then map the alert values to the YTD Cost Column and the As Percentage of Target to the YTD Budget column, because we want to alert when the TYD Cost approaches the budget figure.

Next, set the alert thresholds to Min-90%, 90%-110% and 110% to Maximum and assign a green tick, amber exclamation and red cross.

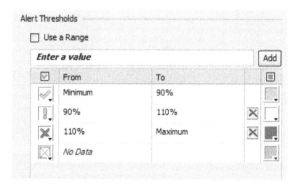

Remember to disable auto colours and set the **Low Values are Good** radio button.

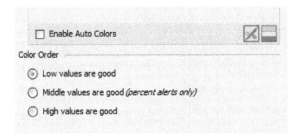

Your chart should update in real time to show the effect of the alerts:

Category	Q1	Q2		YTD Cost		YTD Budget	
Office Rental	3000	➡	3000	!	6000	6000	▲
Equipment Rental	1000	🔺	1200	!	2200	2000	
Marketing	1500	🔺	2000	✓	3500	4000	
Legal Fees	950	🔻	200	✖	1150	500	
Electricity	650	🔺	700	✖	1350	1200	
Communications	850	🔺	1000	!	1850	2000	
Fuel	1500	🔻	1000	✖	2500	2000	▼

Expenditure v Budget

You should be able to see that if the YTD Cost is below 90% of the YTD budget, then it gets a green tick, as in our Marketing example. If it is within 10% either side of the budget then an amber alert is raised, as in our Office Rental and if it is over 10% higher than budget, a red cross is displayed, for example in our legal fees.

Finally we need to set up the coloured background on any figure that had exceeded budget and we will apply this to the YTD Budget value column.

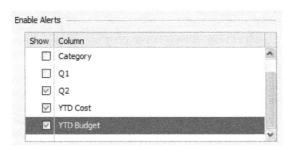

This time however, for each value we only want one of two states, either highlighted (if the cost exceeds the budget) or not highlighted (if the cost does not exceed the budget). So we will select the budget column as our values to compare the the YTD Cost as the values that we are comparing to.

Next we set two ranges, minimum to 100% and 100% to Maximum. So what we are currently saying is if the YTD budget is between minimum i.e. zero and 100% of the YTD cost e.g. 2000, then it will be highlighted by the first row.

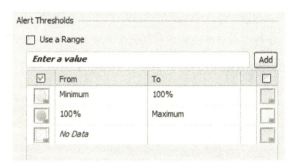

For our office rental which is a YTD Cost of 2200 against a budget of 2000, the budget is between zero and 100% of YTD Cost (2200), but rather than wanting this to show as green we want it to be picked out as an exception alert, so we much switch the colour order to say **High Values are Good**

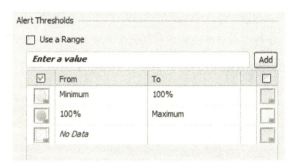

159

Next we disable **Auto Colours**

and for both icons on the left of the **Alert Threshold** rows
we select the **No Icon** option, because all we want to do is
colour the background.

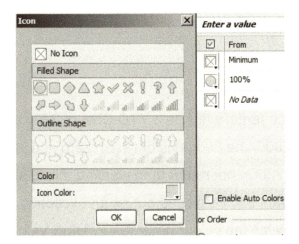

Then over on the right of the row, we select a red background for the Minimum row and a plain white background for the 100% - Maximum row.

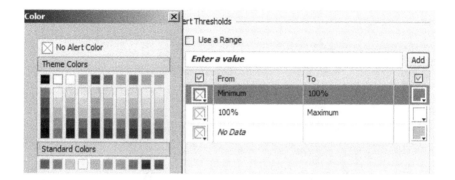

Now when you preview your Scorecard, you will see that anywhere the YTD cost exceeds the budget, the budget figure is highlighted in red.

Expenditure v Budget

Category	Q1	Q2		YTD Cost	YTD Budget	
Office Rental	3000	➡	3000	! 6000	6000	
Equipment Rental	1000	↗	1200	! 2200	2000	
Marketing	1500	↗	2000	✓ 3500	4000	
Legal Fees	950	↘	200	✖ 1150	500	
Electricity	650	↗	700	✖ 1350	1200	
Communications	850	↗	1000	! 1850	2000	
Fuel	1500	↘	1000	✖ 2500	2000	

Notice also that the Scorecard is an active component, so you can enable it for insertion, so that when a user clicks on a row you can perform drills. This is common across many of the components as per our example way back at the beginning of the book.

Maps

For this example we are going to use a spreadsheet of data containing all the US population data by zip code. This is available in the public domain from:

http://www.unitedstateszipcodes.org/zip-code-database/

When you have the file (which comes as a csv), open it in Excel and save it as an XLS file. Notice that the database has multiple rows per state and for our map we are interested in the population by state, so since we need to group and summarise the spreadsheet, we will import it to SQL Server (or whatever database you are using) and then you can either create a web service to provide the data or perform your grouping and summarisation in SQL and place the result back in Excel.

There are a number of unwanted columns in the file, some of which cause a problem when we import them to SQL Server, so remove these first, leaving just the

ZIP, TYPE, PRIMARY_CITY, STATE, LATITUDE, LONGITUDE, COUNTRY and ESTIMATED_POPULATION.

	A	B	C	D	E	F	G	H	I
1	zip	type	primary_city	state	latitude	longitude	country	estimated_population	
2	501	UNIQUE	Holtsville	NY	40.81	-73.04	US	384	
3	544	UNIQUE	Holtsville	NY	40.81	-73.04	US	0	
4	601	STANDARI	Adjuntas	PR	18.16	-66.72	US	0	
5	602	STANDARI	Aguada	PR	18.38	-67.18	US	0	
6	603	STANDARI	Aguadilla	PR	18.43	-67.15	US	0	
7	604	PO BOX	Aguadilla	PR	18.43	-67.15	US	0	
8	605	PO BOX	Aguadilla	PR	18.43	-67.15	US	0	
9	606	STANDARI	Maricao	PR	18.18	-66.98	US	0	
10	610	STANDARI	Anasco	PR	18.28	-67.14	US	0	
11	611	PO BOX	Angeles	PR	18.28	-66.79	US	0	
12	612	STANDARI	Arecibo	PR	18.45	-66.73	US	0	
13	613	PO BOX	Arecibo	PR	18.45	-66.73	US	0	
14	614	PO BOX	Arecibo	PR	18.45	66.73	US	0	

Next, set up a new database and import the spreadsheet.

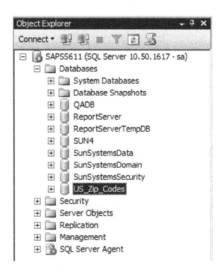

If you are using SQL Server as I was, then the import steps will be similar to the following:

Right click on the database name and select **Tasks / Import Data.** Select Excel as the Data Source, browse to the spreadsheet and ensure **First row has column names** is checked.

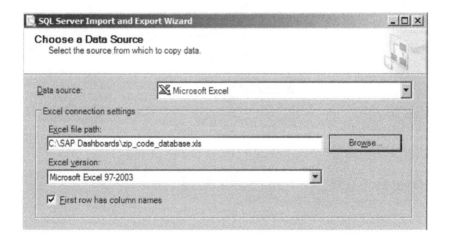

The destination will be your newly created database.

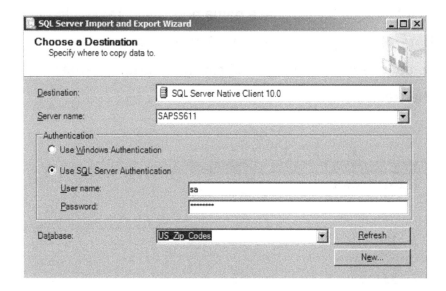

Select to copy data from one or more tables or views.

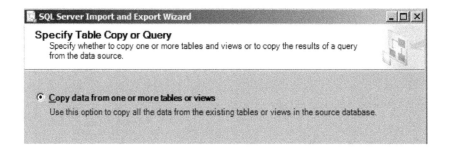

Accept the default mappings as SQL Server will ensure these are logical for importing your spreadsheet.

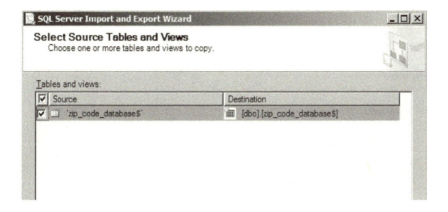

You should see that 42522 rows are imported.

Next use SQL similar to the following to select the total population per state. Either build this into a data connect web service or copy the result directly into the spreadsheet inside Dashboards.

```
select SUM(estimated_population) as population, state
from zip_code_database
where estimated_population > 0
group by state
```

	A	B
1	state	population
2	AK	553665
3	AL	3671857
4	AR	2134523
5	AZ	4437076
6	CA	38218556

Be sure to swap the state field to the left hand side and the population figures to the right. The fully populated spreadsheet is available as part of the example dashboard that you can download from the companion web site.

Now pick up the USA (Continental) map from the palette and place it on the canvass.

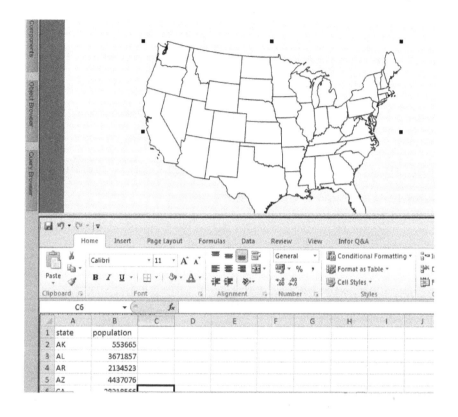

Now to map the map to the spreadsheet. Over in the

properties panel you will see a field call **Region Keys**

Region Keys

If you click the edit button on the far right, you will see a list of the built in region keys for the map component. On the left it shows the name of the region and on the right it shows the Key value that the map will look for in the spreadsheet to correspond to the region. Of course you will be thinking by now, "my spreadsheet has 2 letter region codes and the map component requires the full state name!"

Well, the good news is that we can type over the Region Key with our own values, i.e. those which match the spreadsheet.

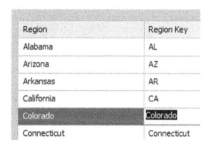

Region	Region Key
Alabama	AL
Arizona	AZ
Arkansas	AR
California	CA
Colorado	Colorado
Connecticut	Connecticut

Of course this can be a bit laborious, so the even better news is that you can simply import the region keys to the component, from the spreadsheet.

To do this, select the import button next to the Region Key field and map It to the list of regions on the spreadsheet.

Region Keys

Sheet1!$A$2:$A$50

Now when you look at the Region Keys list, you will see that they are fully mapped.

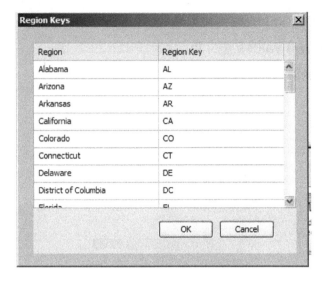

The only thing to look out for is that the region keys on your spreadsheet correspond to the order of the region keys in the Region Key list. In other words, the key values on your spreadsheet must be in the same order as the list of regions in the key List.

Next you need to map the display data, i.e. all the data that will be displayed on the map, for each region. Note that this mapping has to include the region key list on the left, so you will be mapping to 2 columns as shown.

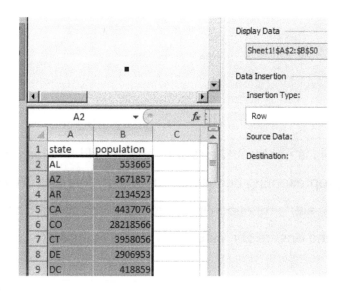

Now when you preview your map, you will see that when you hover your mouse over a region, the population figure is displayed.

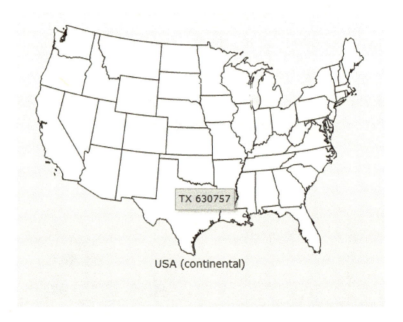

USA (continental)

So far this is not terribly exciting, so lets add a splash of colour, representing density of population. We can do this using the alerts functionality, so to start with select **Enable Alerts** and ensure **By Value** and **Use a Range** are checked.

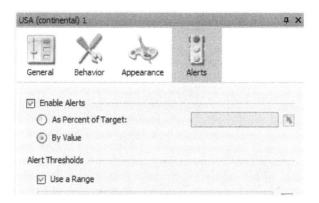

This means that we will be setting a range of values on the spreadsheet to act as our alert values, in other words if the population is between one value and another, then we will set it to a certain colour. It is easy to set the range, simply use the range selector and map it to the list of population values.

With auto colours enabled, the system sets up the entire range of population values for us and assigns a colour.

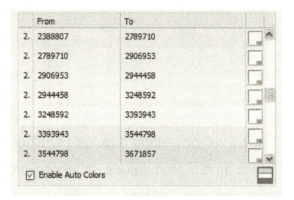

	From	To		
2.	2388807	2789710		
2.	2789710	2906953		
2.	2906953	2944458		
2.	2944458	3248592		
2.	3248592	3393943		
2.	3393943	3544798		
2.	3544798	3671857		
☑ Enable Auto Colors				

If you are not partial to the default primary colours, you can click the **Colour Selector** and chose a different palette, or even create your own.

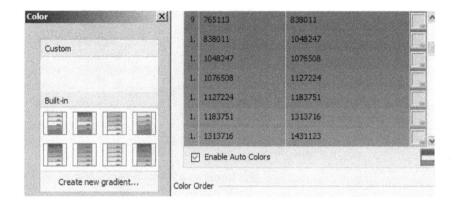

Now when you preview the map, you will see that the population density is colour coded.

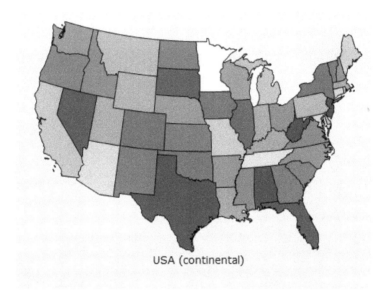

USA (continental)

Of course, maps like many other components are interactive, so they can be used to make selections and pass those selections on to other controls. As an example, lets say we had the influenza figures for each state in a particular year. We don't but we can make up some numbers using a simple formula in Excel.

Using the random number generator, we can set up a formula like this and apply it to a new column, thus giving us a randomized influenza figure for each state.

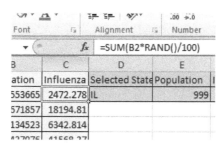

With that done, we need to set the insert properties of the map. Under the **General Properties** set the **Data Insertion** to **Row** and map the source data to the three columns of the state, population and influenza figures table.

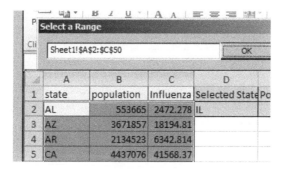

Next, set the destination to a new set of cells.

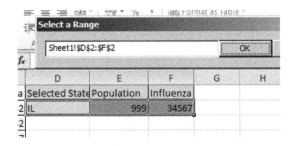

When the user selects a state from the map, the values for State, population and influenza, will be copied into the new cells and, for the purposes of a simple example, we can base a gauge control on this area.

As usual, place a gauge control on the canvass and give it a name. Also name the indicator and map it to the Influenza figure in the table that will contain the results of the user selection.

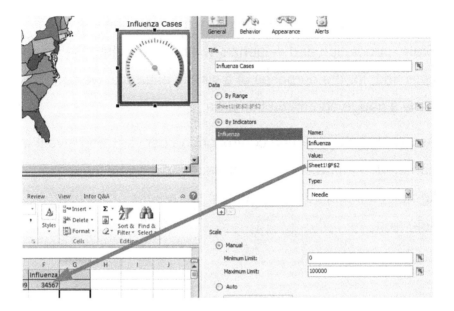

Also, set the **Scale**, in my case I know that the maximum will be 100,000 cases in any one state, so I set the scale from zero to 100,000.

184

To give it a bit of colour I have set the alert to be as a percentage of the maximum value.

Now when you select a state, the number of Influenza cases are displayed on the gauge.

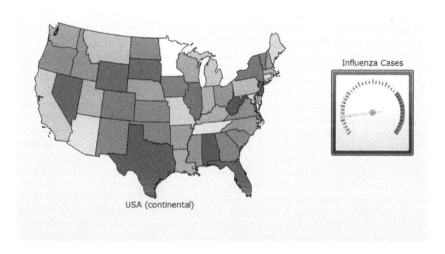

The great thing about gauges though, is that they can contain more than one range of data. So lets say we also knew the average number of flu cases in a year, then we could set a second needle on the gauge to show this.

First of all, add another value to the spreadsheet, showing the average annual cases.

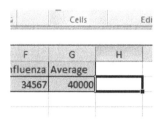

Now use the + button to add another needle to the gauge and map it to the new average value cell.

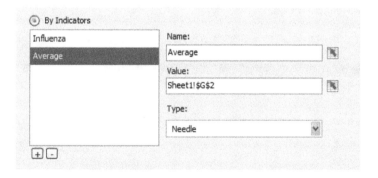

In the appearance section of the control, set the influenza and average values to appear.

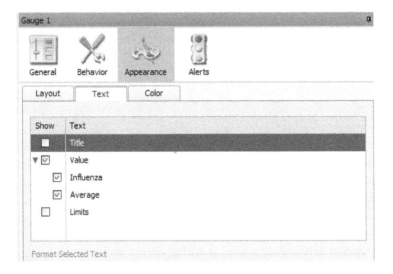

Then finally, in the colour section, set a different colour for the Average needle.

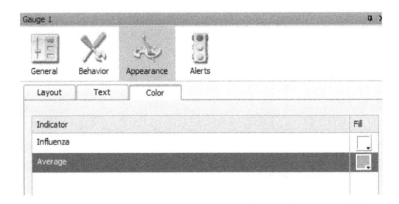

And set the **Frame Colour** to white, so that the labels can be seen clearly over the border.

Now when you preview your map, you get to see the average Influenza figure and the specific figure for the selected state, on the dial. So now you can plan your winter vacation with the lowest risk of catching flu!

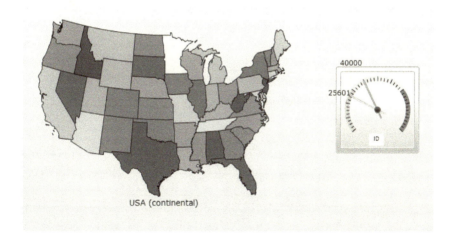

USA (continental)

One thing you may notice, is that due to the random number calculation that we are using, the influenza figures can

189

sometimes have a lot of numbers after the decimal point. This is easy to fix using the number formatting function on the gauge control.

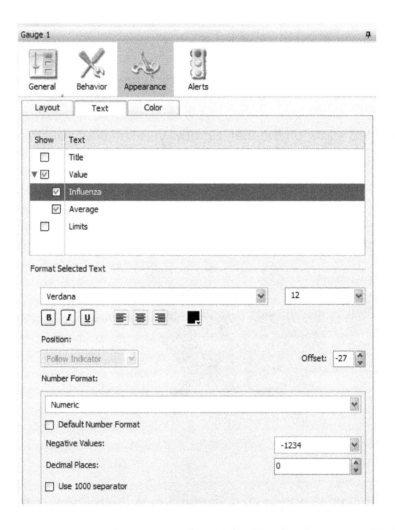

As a finishing touch, on my gauge I added the state code in a label.

Publishing Dashboards

By now you may be thinking, "So I can produce all these fancy dashboards, but how do I publish them to my user base and take all the credit?". Well as with most things to do with this software, that is pretty straightforward too.

I am publishing my dashboards on Microsoft Internet Information Services (IIS) but you can use any web server, since published Dashboards are simply Flash SWF files, which run in a web browser.

If you are running IIS, then you will be able to access the IIS Manager from the start menu on windows:

A number of web sites can be configured to run in this environment, mine is just sitting in the Default Web Site area. You will also notice that this is where the web services that were created with DataConnect are sitting too.

If you right click the **Default Web Site** item, and the **Explore** you will see the files contained in the web root area. Make a note of the path to this folder from the address bar.

Next, in Dashboards, select **File / Export / HTML**

Provide a name for your HTML file and save it to the location you copied in the previous step.

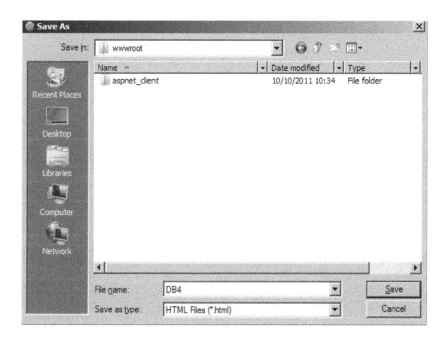

You will see that the HTML and SWF (Flash) files are created.

Now to view your handiwork, just point a browser at the website location. The default web site on a local server is on address http://localhost or IP 127.0.0.1 – follow this with the name of the file you created and you should see your flash chart in the browser.

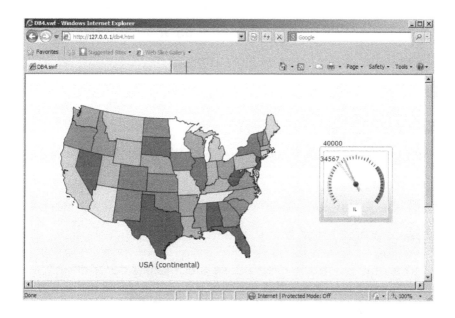

Creating a Menu

In an organisation you may well have several dashboards that you wish to give your users access to. You could put them all on one dashboard and use a tab control to switch between them, but this would mean that the web browser would have to load all the dashboards and data connections at the beginning of the session, making the startup time potentially quite long.

It may be a better idea to have a menu dashboard from which the individual dashboards can be loaded. Of course you could do that in pure HTML, with hyperlinks, but now we have the technology to do it within Dashboards itself, we can present a nice Flash based menu to the user!

Start a new Dashboard and drag a container component on to it, then give it an appropriate title in a label.

Dashboards for Beginners - Example Menu

Next add a URL button for each dashboard that you wish to call from your menu.

URL Button

You can also ad some descriptive text to guide your users.

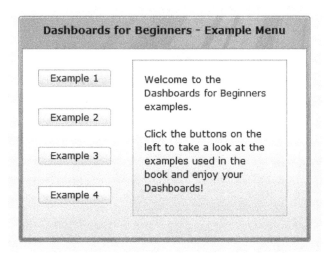

In the properties of the buttons, just add the URL to the individual dashboards. Naturally, if your dashboards are hosted on an internal server, you would put that server address, rather than the localhost address, so that the Dashboards could be accessed from any client computer on your network!

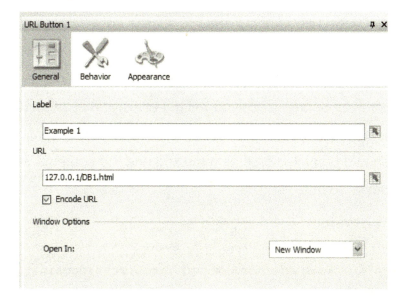

Note: if your data sources need to access data from any other domain than the one they are hosted on, the you will need to place a cross domain policy file in the root of the foreign web server. If not you will get an error message when attempting to access the data. A cross domain policy file should be called crossdomain.xml and the contents will be similar to this:

```
<?xml version="1.0"?>

<!DOCTYPE cross-domain-policy SYSTEM
"http://www.macromedia.com/xml/dtds/cross-domain-
policy.dtd ">

<cross-domain-policy>

<allow-http-request-headers-from domain="*"
headers="*" secure="false" />

<allow-access-from domain="*" secure="false" />
</cross-domain-policy>
```

This may even be the case if you are testing your dashboards on a single web server, because you may launch the home page or menu of your site from 127.0.0.1 yet there may be internal links between the menu and sub-pages, which refer to the web server by its DNS name. Placing a crossdomain.xml file in the root of the web server should solve this issue.

For more details on cross domain policy please see the Adobe web site, since this is a security restriction imposed by the Flash player.

Conclusion

Thank you for choosing Dashboards for Beginners, it has been my pleasure to create this quick start guide to help you on your way to Dashboard excellence. Hopefully it has been a fun and enjoyable experience for you, whilst at the same time helping you to feel comfortable with the product and become able to generate decent looking results in a short space of time.

Don't forget that you can get access to all the examples from this book at my web site http://www.Bappoo.com

I am always happy to receive feedback from my readers so feel free to ping me an email to Paul@Bappoo.com to let me know what you thought of the book and how you are getting on with Dashboards.

I am particularly interested in seeing examples of how you have implemented the system and what you are doing with it, possibly even featuring a case study on my site.

Finally, I also have a few books out about Business Intelligence and Reporting Tools (BIRT), which is an open source (and therefore free) reporting and business intelligence system. BIRT can deliver some great functionality and would be a great companion product to work with Dashboards for when you need an environment in which to host your Dashboards or for when you need to produce listings or documents based on data from your dashboards.

Details of my books are below and you can find them at http://www.Bappoo.com

BIRT for Maximo

This comprehensive self paced training course on using BIRT to create and modify reports for Maximo will teach you all you need to know to get immediate results from the new report writer for Maximo version 7, in just a couple of days.

Then it will provide a handy reference for you to use whilst working with BIRT on your Maximo reporting projects.

Rather than outsourcing your reporting requirements to expensive consultants or undertaking lengthy and costly training courses, working through this workbook is quick and easy with step by step instructions and screenshots to guide you every step of the way.

The main topics covered are:

Installing BIRT for Maximo

Formatting Reports

Sorting, grouping and aggregating data

Creating reports that use parameters

Writing expressions and calculated fields

Building reports that contain sub-reports

Joining different data sets

Creating charts

Creating hyperlinks and drill down functionality

Importing reports to Maximo

Creating and modifying Query Based Reports

Printed in full A4 size, packed with examples, large, easy to read screen shots, step by step instructions and guided exercises, this workbook can be used again and again, as a self study guide or as course notes to use when you run your own training courses in house or for clients plus you always have the full backup and support from the dedicated BIRT forum and the new guides and tutorials that are always being released at www.BIRTReporting.com

See inside the course at: http://www.birtreporting.com/BIRTTraining.html

BIRT for Beginners

This book presents an overview of the open source BIRT tools and the commercial enhancements available from Actuate, including...

Eclipse BIRT Designer, Actuate BIRT Designer, iServer Express, Interactive BIRT viewer, Actuate BIRT Studio, BIRT Spreadsheet Designer

With walkthrough tutorials of the main features, including screenshots, from installation through data selection to formatting reports and fully graphical Flash charting this book will have you creating your own reports from scratch in only a couple of hours. If you are too busy to spend days learning software and want tangible results fast then BIRT For Beginners is for you.

When you buy the book you will automatically get access to the readers section of this web site which includes BIRT report request forms that you can distribute to your end users, extra chapters in PDF format and an ever growing library of reports, tutorials, reviews, tips & tricks.

BIRT by Example

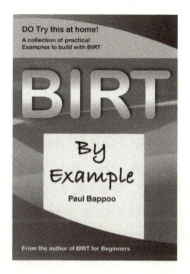

Packed with real life examples, taken from a life on the road, Paul brings his latest fun and inspirational guide to learning BIRT to fruition. Not only can this book teach you BIRT quickly and easily, with lots of practical, step by step examples, but it is also a darn good read, says Paul's mum. Admittedly she doesn't know much about software so you may just have to delve into these pages yourself to learn: Report Templates, Libraries and Master Pages. Switching between databases dynamically. BIRT with Oracle. Applying style sheets to BIRT reports. How to debug your BIRT JavaScript. How to hide empty fields. Using a stored procedure as a data set. How to edit, insert and delete records from a database with BIRT. Using web services as a data source. A Twitter feed built in BIRT. Building reports into Java Server Pages. Installing BIRT on Ubuntu and more. Also get to find out where the worlds best B&B is and how far you need to travel to see the sand dunes in the cover photos!

Index

Alerts..............123, 138, 147, 176

Backgrounds................38, 98, 99

Bubble Chart.......................... 108

Canvas.......................................36

Column Chart 48, 100

Combo box 62

Components...........38, 47, 48, 100

Containers.................................99

Data Source.....................43, 165

DataConnect. .14, 56, 60, 143, 193

Dials........................ 123, 135, 136

Drill................11, 82, 84, 162, 206

Excel...11, 12, 31, 35, 40, 41, 163, 165, 180, 204

Filter......................... 22, 55, 82, 88

FlyNet..................9, 13, 14, 21, 43

Gauges...........................123, 136

Image.................................... 3, 99

Import Spreadsheet 35

Label 63, 70, 71, 76, 99, 106, 129, 189

Labels......63, 70, 71, 76, 99, 106, 129, 189

Line chart 123, 129

Line Charts..............................123

List...........................105, 106, 175

Manage Connections................35

Map 35, 39, 45, 46, 68, 73, 75, 76, 78, 103, 109, 110, 113, 118, 122, 129, 133, 135, 136, 143, 148, 155, 163, 167, 170, 171, 172, 173, 175, 176, 177, 180, 181, 183, 187, 189

Menu......34, 36, 43, 192, 198, 199

Object Browser.........................38

OHLC.............................. 102, 103

Oracle................................12, 209

Parameter. .35, 65, 66, 70, 88, 206

Pie chart 11, 82, 89, 90, 92, 93, 94, 95, 96, 97, 100

Play Selector............114, 119, 120

Preview......25, 37, 53, 54, 69, 70, 121, 151, 162, 176, 180, 189

Publishing...............................192

Query...17, 21, 22, 24, 25, 26, 28, 42, 43, 55, 56, 65, 70, 82, 83, 86, 87, 88, 89, 207

Quick Views.............................37

SalesByProduct.......21, 70, 73, 86

SAP...................................... 11, 12

Scorecards.............................141

Selector. .46, 62, 89, 93, 115, 122, 143, 177

Sliders................................ 123, 133

Spreadsheet Table.................... 115

SQL 12, 13, 17, 19, 21, 22, 25, 65, 163, 165, 167, 169

SunSystems............................5, 21

Tab....................................101, 115

Text Input................................ 111

Toolbars...............................34, 37

URL................43, 44, 60, 199, 200

Visibility............................... 90, 92

Web service 13, 17, 19, 21, 26, 27, 28, 42, 43, 44, 45, 46, 47, 54, 57, 65, 163, 169, 193, 209

WSDL.....................28, 43, 44, 60

Xcelsius....................................... 11
................111, 135, 136, 191, 198

www.ingramcontent.com/pod-product-compliance
Lightning Source LLC
Chambersburg PA
CBHW051236050326
40689CB00007B/941